THE EVERYTHING KIDS' PUZZLE BOOK

Mazes, Word Games, Puzzles & More! Hours of Fun!

Jennifer A. Ericsson &
Beth L. Blair

Adams Media Corporation
Holbrook, Massachusetts

D1417684

WHAT PARENTS AND TEACHERS SAY

"*The Everything® Kids' Puzzle Book* is fun, challenging, and educational. The wide variety of activities kept my daughters (ages 7 and 9) entertained for hours on a snowy afternoon. A vital book for the entertainment section of any parents' library, excellent for travel. A great gift to give and receive."
Lynn Favreau, RN, mother, homeschooling parent

"A great resource that lives up to its name. This book has everything—from fun time fillers and brain stretchers to activities that reinforce basic learning skills. It's sure to be a hit with elementary-aged students."
Molly Braun
2nd Grade Teacher
St. Paul, MN

An Everything® Series Book.
Everything® is a registered trademark of Adams Media Corporation.

Published by Adams Media Corporation
260 Center Street, Holbrook, MA 02343. U. S.A.

ISBN: 1-58062-323-9

Printed in the United States of America.

J I H G F E D C

This publication is designed to provide accurate and authoritative information with regard to the subject matter covered. It is sold with the understanding that the publisher is not engaged in rendering legal, accounting, or other professional advice. If legal advice or other expert assistance is required, the services of a competent professional person should be sought.
— From a *Declaration of Principles* jointly adopted by a Committee of the American Bar Association and a Committee of Publishers and Associations

Text design and illustrations by Beth L. Blair.

Puzzle Power software by Centron Software Technologies, Inc. was used to create the puzzle grids for "Wordsearch," "Quote Fall," "KrissKross," and "Cross Sums" puzzles.

This book is available at quantity discounts for bulk purchases.
For information, call 1-800-872-5627.

Visit our Web site at www.adamsmedia.com

CONTENTS

INTRODUCTION

If you're between the ages of eight and twelve, we know there are puzzles in this book you will love. Maybe you're wacky for word play. We've got it. Maybe you think picture puzzles are positively peachy. They're here. Maybe you're cuckoo for crisscrosses or think mazes are marvelous. Look inside. This book isn't called the *Everything® Kids' Puzzle Book* for nothing!

Not only did we cram as many kinds of puzzles into this book as possible, we also came up with all types of themes to interest you. You'll find everything from Pets to Pizza, Music to Monsters, Camping to Computers. And wherever there was room, we stuffed in fascinating facts and Fast n' Funny jokes.

To make things even more exciting, there are a couple of puzzles that run through the whole book. First, watch for Mervin the mouse. He's hidden somewhere on each and every spread (the two pages you have open at any one time). Sometimes he's easy to spot—but not always! You will also notice that there are random white letters mixed among the dark ones. These are not mistakes, but are clues to the White Out! puzzle found in the "What a Great Idea!" section.

So, flip the book open and dive right in. We wish you many happy puzzling hours ahead!

Jennifer A. Ericsson
Beth L. Blair

PILES OF PETS

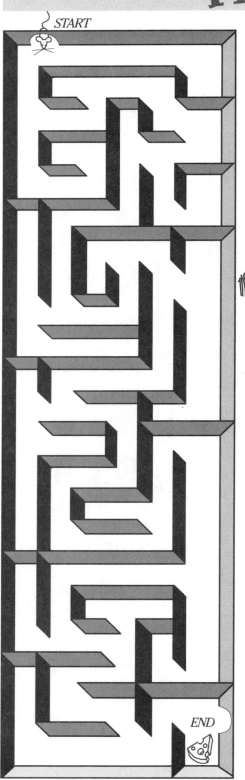

START

END

Mouse Maze

Mervin is a very curious mouse, and he smells cheese! Can you get Mervin through the maze, left, to his favorite snack?

Pet Groupie

A groupie is a type of puzzle that has only one clue—the word provided. Your job is to figure out the other words that belong in the puzzle. Hint: Some of the animals pictured are clues!

P A R A K E E T

Mouse on the Loose!

Oh no! Mervin went right by the cheese and out of the maze! Look for him throughout the rest of this book. He'll show up at least once on every two pages, and sometimes twice! Look carefully—Mervin can be *very* good at hiding!

2

Kitty Compounds

Can you figure out the compound words in each of these pictures?

C A T _ _ _ _ _

=YAKITTY=
> YAKITTY
> YAKITTY

Fast 'n' Funny
What does the vet keep outside his front door?

A welcome mutt!

C A T _ _ _ _
OUCH

C A T _ _ _ _

Animal Antics

Try these tongue twisters!

Dirty dogs dig deep.

Seven slinky snakes sneak snacks.

Five fancy fish finish fixing fins.

Many mice make much music.

C A T _ _ _ _

C A T _ _ _ _

C A T _ _ _ _
Z Z Z Z

3

CLOTHES CLOSET

Hat Hamper

To fill this hamper with hats, think of a name and a describing word that both start with the same first letter. Try your family's, friend's, or even your pet's names! A sample hat has been done for you.

ANNIE's hat is an *ARTSY* hat.

Use this space to draw the hat that goes with your name!

Hamper Maze

START

FINISH

_____'s hat is a _____ hat.

_____'s hat is a _____ hat.

_____'s hat is a _____ hat.

_____'s hat is a _____ hat.

What Would You Wear?

Dressing up, dressing down, getting dressed to go to town. In this grid, can you find fifty items you could wear? Words always run in a straight line, but they may go horizontally, vertically, or diagonally. They may also run backward or forward. When you are finished, read the unused letters from left to right and you will discover what is the most valuable pair of pants in the whole world.

```
P A V J A C K E T I W N S C R O W N
T I E E T A A G E A S K C O S S E C
B S N A O P N D T S H A A I G G N D
A T P N A E I C E R O B R N N O F L
T R E S V I H R J E O A F I I W S T
H O N S U N D E R W E A R K R N L I
R H T S G N I G G E L H I I R A L G
O S S R E P P I L S T C B B A T A H
B B N O S T T S S T W E B N E A R T
E O E V T L T R I H S H O E S O E S
U O A Y E N F R P I R V N E T C V T
N T K B A S E O I E H O U E S A O S
I S E P A C T C P K N C L O G D D W
F O R K L K L M K A S E V O L G R E
O S S T N H U A T L C S H P A R K A
R A A A R J D A T A A O B E S U I T
M I T T E N S O R O H C N O P L I E
C O S T U M E B E V S W E A T S E R
```

WORD LIST

bathrobe	coat	jumper	ribbon	suit
belt	costume	leggings	ring	sweater
bikini	crown	mask	scarf	sweats
boa	dress	mittens	shirt	tank top
boots	earrings	necklace	shoes	tie
bow	gloves	overalls	shorts	tights
bracelet	gown	pants	skirt	underwear
cap	hat	parka	slippers	uniform
cape	jacket	pin	sneakers	vest
clog	jeans	poncho	socks	watch

What's Different?

Can you find the seven things that are different between these two coats?

Fast 'n' Funny

What kind of coat won't keep you warm?

A coat of paint.

PUZZLING PRESIDENTS

Capitol Maze

ENTER

Capitol Confusion

During the Civil War, the Capitol building was used for many different purposes. Read the list below and see if you can guess which are correct.

1. soldiers' barracks
2. hospital
3. bakery
4. stable
5. blacksmith shop

Hidden Presidents

Six presidents are hiding in the windows of the capitol building, below. Can you figure out which one is in each? Part of their first name is on the top line and part of their last name is on the bottom. A list of presidents is given, but not all of them are used!

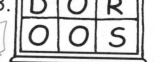

President List

Theodore Roosevelt
Thomas Jefferson
Ronald Reagan
George Washington
Harry S. Truman
Bill Clinton
Abraham Lincoln
Dwight Eisenhower
Richard M. Nixon
John F. Kennedy

1.
O	R	G
A	S	H

2.
A	H	A
C	O	L

3.
D	O	R
O	O	S

4.
J	O	H
N	E	D

5.
C	H	A
I	X	O

6.
I	L	L
N	T	O

EXIT

Rebus for President!

Use this combination of pictures and letters to spell out the names of two well known presidents.

1. D +   + ZN +

2. G +  + G

Quotable Quote

Answer as many clues as you can, and fill the letters you have into the grid. Work back and forth between the quotation box and clues until you can read this famous line once said by John F. Kennedy, the thirty-fifth President of the United States.

1	2	3		4	5		6	7		8	9	10	11	12	13		14	15	16	17	18	19	20	21	22
	23	24	25		26	27	28		29	30	31	32		33	34	35	36		37	38	39	40	41	42	43
	44	45	46		47	48		49	50	51		52	53	54		55	56	57		58	59	60	61		62
63	64		65	66	67		68	69		70	71	72		73	74	75	76		77	78	79	80	81	82	83

A. Person, place, or thing
$\overline{67}\ \overline{34}\ \overline{54}\ \overline{40}$

B. To fasten
$\overline{10}\ \overline{50}\ \overline{65}\ \overline{25}$

C. To hurry
$\overline{72}\ \overline{39}\ \overline{24}\ \overline{59}$

D. What a cow chews
$\overline{19}\ \overline{75}\ \overline{68}$

E. Adult male human
$\overline{15}\ \overline{1}\ \overline{21}$

F. Caterpillar case
$\overline{44}\ \overline{12}\ \overline{37}\ \overline{5}\ \overline{71}\ \overline{80}$

G. Building in which people live
$\overline{30}\ \overline{48}\ \overline{79}\ \overline{56}\ \overline{9}$

H. Opposite of night
$\overline{47}\ \overline{14}\ \overline{33}$

I. To move through the air with wings
$\overline{49}\ \overline{11}\ \overline{43}$

J. A plaything
$\overline{32}\ \overline{69}\ \overline{52}$

K. Pull suddenly
$\overline{83}\ \overline{20}\ \overline{2}\ \overline{57}$

L. A large number
$\overline{6}\ \overline{31}\ \overline{46}\ \overline{73}$

M. Sound a dog makes
$\overline{13}\ \overline{53}\ \overline{38}\ \overline{70}$

N. To attempt
$\overline{81}\ \overline{36}\ \overline{62}$

O. Abrupt
$\overline{77}\ \overline{35}\ \overline{17}\ \overline{61}$

P. Unhappy
$\overline{22}\ \overline{66}\ \overline{3}$

Q. In another direction
$\overline{60}\ \overline{29}\ \overline{55}\ \overline{7}$

R. Part of plant that grows underground
$\overline{42}\ \overline{78}\ \overline{63}\ \overline{28}$

S. Person trained to care for the sick
$\overline{26}\ \overline{64}\ \overline{76}\ \overline{4}\ \overline{16}$

T. Twelve inches
$\overline{8}\ \overline{74}\ \overline{27}\ \overline{41}$

U. Mixture of gases surrounding Earth
$\overline{45}\ \overline{18}\ \overline{82}$

V. Armed fighting between people
$\overline{58}\ \overline{23}\ \overline{51}$

TUTTI-FRUTTI

Lost Lemons

No wonder Josh looks sour — Jess and his dog Rosie knocked over his lemonade stand! See if you can find the sixteen lemon slices splashed throughout the picture below.

Fruit Salad

Unscramble these words to find ingredients for a fruit salad.

1. RUEBELRIEBS   _ _ _ _ _ _ _ _ _ _
2. LEMTERAWNO   _ _ _ _ _ _ _ _ _ _
3. TALCNOPUAE   _ _ _ _ _ _ _ _ _ _
4. PESPAL   _ _ _ _ _ _
5. NASABAN   _ _ _ _ _ _ _
6. PRGAES   _ _ _ _ _ _

Serve 'em Up

Cross out all the odd numbers and capital letters. The remaining numbers and letters will remind you how many servings of fruit you should eat each day!

B 2 1 C 7 1
3 F † X 5 o
V 1 7 Y 4 K

Fast 'n' Funny
What do you call two bananas?

A pair of slippers!

Positively Peachy

Fill in the missing letters to find plenty of fruits that start with the letter P and one hard word that is found in the center of many fruits!

Tropical Maze
Find your way through this prickly pineapple.

9

FINISH

Money Maze

START · Can you find the dollar sign in the maze? · FINISH

Money Match

Draw a line from each denomination of money to the person whose portrait appears on it. Hint: Some names are used more than once.

penny	Ulysses S. Grant
nickel	Thomas Jefferson
dime	George Washington
quarter	Alexander Hamilton
$1.00	Abraham Lincoln
$2.00	George Washington
$5.00	Thomas Jefferson
$10.00	Abraham Lincoln
$20.00	Franklin D. Roosevelt
$50.00	Benjamin Franklin
$100.00	Andrew Jackson

Loose Change

Cross out every D-O-L-L-A-R in the grid below, and the remaining letters will tell you what is your nose's favorite money.

```
d  O  l  L  A  r  D  o  L
L  a  R  C  O  L  l  A  r
l  e  A  r  D  o  N  I  L
O  L  l  A  r  L  a  R  d
I  T  A  r  D  o  L  s  A
```

10

Can I Borrow a Drachma?

Money is called different things in different countries. See if you can fit all of these world currencies into the crisscross grid (use just the money name). We left some M-O-N-E-Y in the grid to get you started.

3 letters:
KIP   (Laos)
LEK   (Albania)
LEV   (Bulgaria)
WON   (Korea)
YEN   (Japan)

4 letters:
BAHT   (Thailand)
BIRR   (Ethiopia)
DONG   (Vietnam)
DRAM   (Armenia)
EURO   (Europe)
LIRA   (Italy)

MARK   (Germany)
PESO   (Chile)
PULA   (Botswana)
RIEL   (Cambodia)
TAKA   (Bangladesh)

5 letters:
COLON   (El Salvador)
DINAR   (Libya)
FRANC   (France)
KRONE   (Denmark)
POUND   (Great Britain)
RUBLE   (Belarus)
RUPEE   (India)
SUCRE   (Ecuador)
ZLOTY   (Poland)

6 letters:
DOLLAR   (United States)
FORINT   (Hungary)
KORUNA   (Czech Republic)
MARKKA   (Finland)

7 letters:
DRACHMA (Greece)
GUILDER (Netherlands)
QUETZAL (Guatemala)

8 letters:
SHILLING (Kenya)

F.Y.I.
Eleven European countries, including France, Germany, and Italy, began using the <u>euro</u> in January, 1999. On July 1, 2002, these countries will change over completely and money like the franc, mark, and lira will no longer be used.

• • • • • • • • • •

Do you know who is the youngest multibillionaire?

Athina Onassis Roussel, grand-daughter of Greek shipping magnate Aristotle Onassis. She inherited an estimated $5 billion in 1988.

11

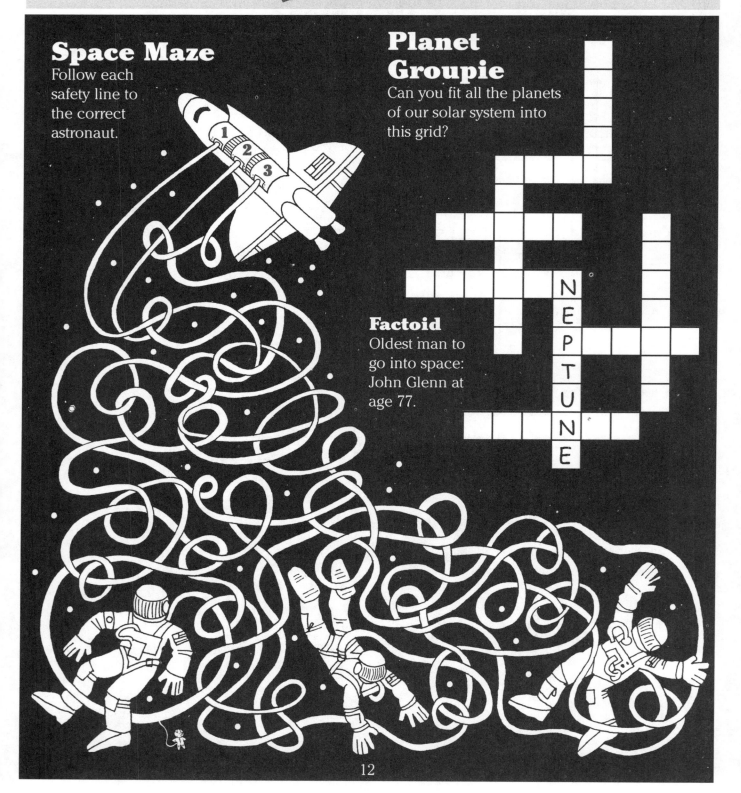

SPACE RACE

Space Maze

Follow each safety line to the correct astronaut.

1
2
3

Planet Groupie

Can you fit all the planets of our solar system into this grid?

N
E
P
T
U
N
E

Factoid

Oldest man to go into space: John Glenn at age 77.

Moon Phase Decoder

Use this decoder to find out how long it takes for the moon to go through all of its phases.

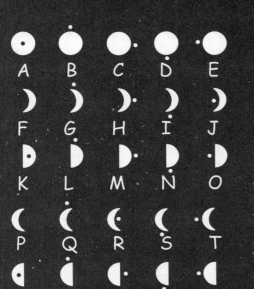

A B C D E
F G H I J
K L M N O
P Q R S T
U V W X Y
Z

One Small Step

Use this combination of astronauts to spell out the name of the first person to walk on the moon.

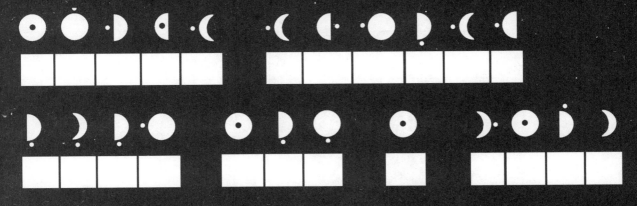

Fast 'n' Funny

Why couldn't the astronaut land on the moon?

Because the moon was full!

Factoid

John Glenn was also the first American to orbit the earth.

The most people in space at once was on March 18, 1995.
— 7 Americans (STS 67 Endeavor)
— 3 Cosmonauts (MIR Space Station)
— 2 Cosmonauts + 1 US Astronaut (Soyuz TM21)

Classic Tic-Tac-Toe

Choose whether you want an X or an O to be your mark. Have a friend, sibling, or parent be the other mark. Taking turns, make your mark in one of the nine 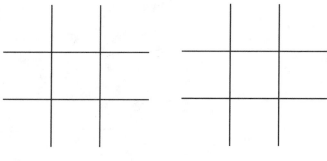 tic-tac-toe squares. The object is to get three of your marks in a row — horizontally, vertically, or diagonally. If you have done this, draw a line through all three marks and yell "Tic-Tac-Toe." You win!

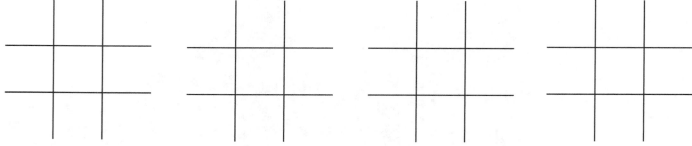

Super Duper Tic-Tac-Toe

In this larger game, each player tries to get three, four, or five marks in a row. You do not win with just one line — try to make as many as you can. Each X or O can be counted more than once if it is included in a different line.

When all the spaces are filled, each player adds up their score:

— 1 point for three marks in a row

— 3 points for four marks in a row

— 5 points for five marks in a row

High score wins!

If you want to play some more, make your own boards on the blank pages at the end of this book.

Classic Hangman

This is a game of mystery words.

To play:

1. Find a partner to play with you. One of you will think up the word (the drawer) and the other will try to guess it (the guesser).

2. The drawer thinks up a word and tells the guesser how many letters it has.

3. The guesser guesses one letter at a time. If the letter is in the word, the drawer writes it in the proper space or spaces. If not, the drawer writes the used letter next to the hangman gallow and draws the head on the hangman.

4. Play continues and a new body part is added to the hangman each time a wrong letter is guessed (stick body, arms, legs, dots for eyes & nose, frown).

To win:

Either the guesser or the drawer can win. If the guesser figures out the word before the hangman is completely drawn, then he wins. But if he doesn't, then the drawer wins. The guesser can also try to solve the word at any time, but automatically loses the game if he or she is wrong.

Oops! The guesser in this game did not guess the word "stand" before the hangman was completed. The guesser loses.

Updating a Classic

Can you think of which current and popular game show is based on Hangman? Need a hint? Buy a vowel!

Wheel of Fortune

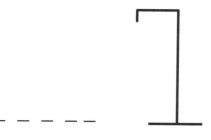

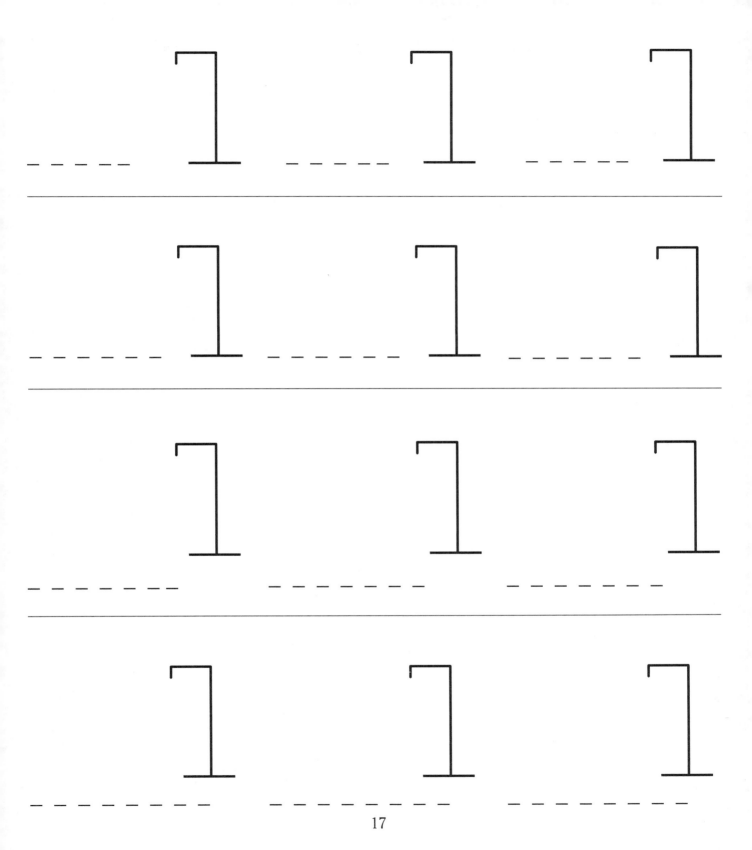

IT TAKES TWO: BOXES

Classic Boxes

Play this game with a friend. Taking turns, each player connects two neighboring dots. Each player uses a different colored pencil. Your line can go up and down or side-to-side, but <u>not</u> diagonally. Continue and try to be the one to close up each square. When you do, write your initials inside the box and take an extra turn. The winner will be the one with the most boxes at the end.

Lotsa Boxes

If you want to play some more, make your own dot grid on the blank pages at the end of this book or on a piece of graph paper.

Not a Lotta Boxes

Tired of playing the usual way? Start a new game and try to make the FEWEST boxes!

Initials___ # of Boxes ___   Initials___ # of Boxes ___

Initials___ # of Boxes ___   Initials___ # of Boxes ___

Initials___ # of Boxes ___   Initials___ # of Boxes ___

Initials ___

# of Boxes ___

Initials ___

# of Boxes ___

Initials ___

# of Boxes ___

Initials ___

# of Boxes ___

Initials ___

# of Boxes ___

Initials ___

# of Boxes ___

Initials ___

# of Boxes ___

Initials ___

# of Boxes ___

Barely Square

A square is flat, and that's that. But just add a few lines and you can create a 3-D cube that's fun to play with!

First, draw a square.

Then draw another square that overlaps the first.

Connect the four corners with straight lines. Now you have a see-through cube.

If you shade the first square you drew, it looks like the cube zooms up to the left.

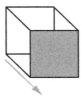

If instead you shade the second square you drew, the cube seems to zip down to the right!

Try shading the sides of the cube. Now you have a cube you can go right through!

How many sides (or faces) does your cube have?

_____

Can you guess the other name for a geometric figure with that many faces?

tetrahedron

hexahedron

octahedron

dodecahedron

Here's a hint:

The first part of the words above tell you the number of faces the geometric figure has.

tetra-   four

hexa-   six

octa-   eight

dodeca-   twelve

ARTSY SMARTSY

Color-a-Message

Color in all the F's, K's and M's and read the remaining letters to see what Johann Wolfgang von Goethe had to say about art.

I F N K M A R M T
K T F H F K E F M
B K E K S T M I S
F G F O F K O F D
K M E N K O U G H

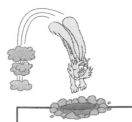

Mixing Colors

Change one letter in each word to create the name of a color. Write the new word in the paint pot below and color the pot to match!

Squiggle Giggles
Draw a car or truck using these 4 lines.

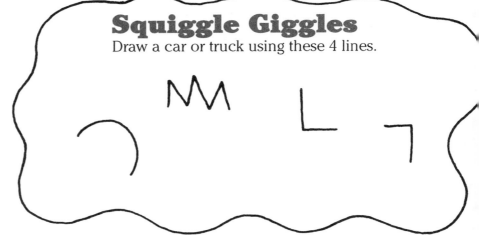

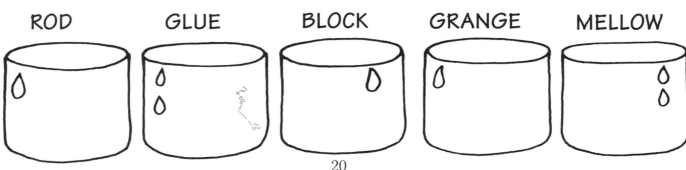

ROD   GLUE   BLOCK   GRANGE   MELLOW

20

Famous Artists

Six famous artists have signed the backs of their paintings, but they wrote too big! Part of their first name is on the top line, and part of their second name is on the bottom line. Can you figure them out?

Possible Artists:
Mary Cassatt
Winslow Homer
Leonardo da Vinci
Pablo Picasso
Paul Cezanne
Vincent van Gogh
Claude Monet
Georgia O'Keefe
Edgar Degas

1. BLO / ICA

2. UDE / NET

3. MAR / SAT

4. EOR / EEF

5. NAR / INC

6. INC / NGO

Same Frames?

The artists are very different, but these frames sure look the same. Try to match the three pairs of frames that are exactly alike.

Squiggle Giggles

Draw an insect using these 4 lines.

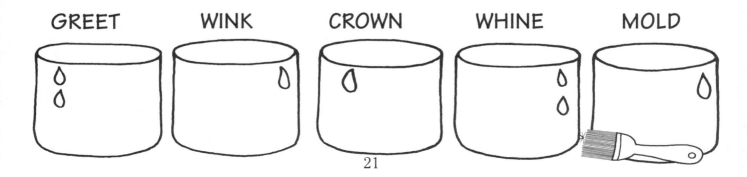

GREET   WINK   CROWN   WHINE   MOLD

LISTEN TO THE MUSIC

Strike Up the Band

How many band instruments can you identify and fit into the grid to the right? One of the instruments left you some O-O-M-P-A as a hint.

Off Key Riddle

Figure out where to put each of the scrambled letters. They all fit in spaces under their own column.

When you fill in the grid, you will have the answer to the following riddle:

What's the difference between a piano and a fish?

P	A	A				N		T		N	E		
C	I	N	T	C	T	B	U	T		Y	I	S	H
Y	O	U	N	O	A	U	N	A	U	F	O	U	A

Classical Composers

The names of six famous composers are hidden on the musical staff. Part of their first name is over part of their last name. Can you figure them out?

1. HAN RAH
2. ETE CHA
3. RAN AYD
4. GAN ART
5. OHA BAC
6. UDW EET

Composer List

Ludwig van Beethoven

Wolfgang Amadeus Mozart

Johann Sebastian Bach

Johannes Brahms

Franz Joseph Haydn

Franz Schubert

Peter Ilyich Tchaikovsky

Name That Tune

Each of the pictures below show the title of a well-known song. Can you guess what each one is?

1.

2.

Read the Music

Using the notes and musical symbols provided, decode this Italian proverb.

D	E	G	H	I	N

R	S	V	W	A	Y

O   SPACE

Fast 'n' Funny
Why did the busy musician spend so much time in bed?

Because he wrote sheet music.

TOOTHFUL GRIN

Whose Teeth Are These?

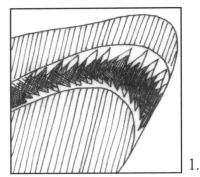

1.

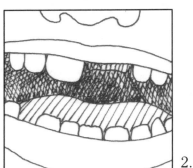

2.

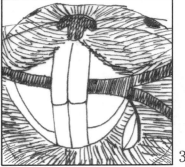

3.

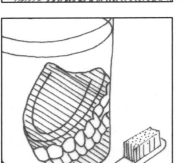

4.

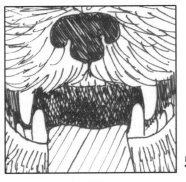

5.

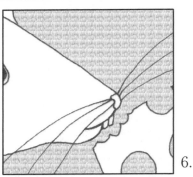

6.

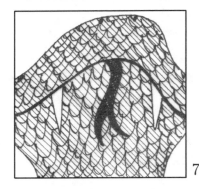

7.

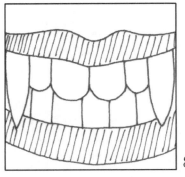

8.

Big Tooth
This is the <u>actual</u> size of one tooth from the eight-ton, 42-foot-long *Gigantosaurus!*

Smiley
What does this computer smiley mean?

: - #

I wear braces!

Fast n' Funny
What has many teeth, but never bites?

A comb!

Tiny Teeth
A pictograph is a very simple drawing — kind of like visual shorthand. Can you guess what this little pictograph (above) shows?

Brace Yourself! Find the path that uses the floss, toothbrush, and toothpaste!

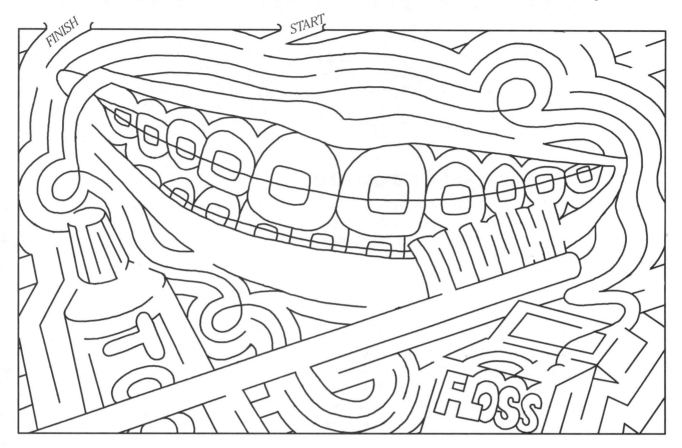

Mystery Words
Fill in the blanks in the following paragraph with words that have to do with the care of your teeth.

_ _ _ _◯_ your teeth after every ◯_ _ _ _ .

_◯_ _ _ often to clean between teeth.

Limit _ _◯_ _ _ to avoid getting cavities.

Visit your _ _ _ _◯_ _ for regular checkups.

Now, unscramble the circled letters to answer this riddle:
**"I'm a road that stretches from left to right.
I'm often paved with pearly white. What am I?"**

25

Follow vines over and under. Which one goes to the snake?

3.

1. 2.

Many Mammals

Find the fifty-six animals hidden in this grid. The sneaky gopher is in twice! Then, read the leftover letters from left to right and find the world's largest animal.

armadillo
ape
badger
bat
bear
beaver
bison
boar
bobcat
caribou
cat
chipmunk
cow
coyote
deer
dog
dolphin
elk
ferret
fox
goat
gopher
gopher
groundhog
horse
human
jaguar
kangaroo

lemming
lynx
lion
manatee
marmot
mole
moose
mouse
muskrat
ocelot
opossum
otter
pig
pika
porcupine
prairie dog
rabbit
raccoon
rat
seal
sheep
shrew
skunk
squirrel
vole
weasel
whale
wolf

```
S J A G U A R N G T H C A R I B O U
Q E F O X W M O O S E H T O L R T L
U D T P N T D O L P H I N A I S T W
I A L H Y A A C R G E P A S O T E E
R A N E L O V C O L E M M I N G R A
R T I R M A L A I W A U U S T E H S
E A E B P I G R L N S N H S E U E E
L C W F H G A L A K E K A D S E A L
A B L T O O O T R V N E W B R O L O
H O S P C D E A N U E E H A U N P K
W B H D E E T R K A R M A D I L L O
E E E D L I O S F H A E E G B T L O
R A E O O R Y N S R G P A E N A D R
A V P O T I O A M V E F E R R E T A
B E A R E A C O K G O H D N U O R G
B R R L T R T W O I H H O R S E A N
I U O N D P O R C U P I N E R E O A
T M D M O U S E T O N S N O S I B K
```

What Are These?

Each of these pictures is a close-up of a different mammal. Can you guess them all?

  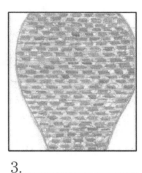  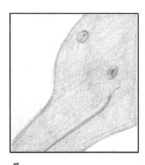

1. _____ 2. _____ 3. _____ 4. _____ 5. _____

 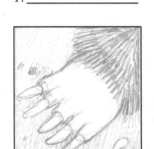   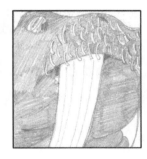

6. _____ 7. _____ 8. _____ 9. _____ 10. _____

Practice Your Paw-menship

 robin

This mysterious note was found on the forest floor. Using the names belonging to the animal tracks provided, can you decipher the message?

bobcat

 bat

woodchuck

vole

otter

fox

chipmunk

 deer

marten

gopher

 muskrat

Can you play baseball later? ___-lend you his ___? We'll ___ pizza, too. Tell your mom we ___ be home by six.

Later,

27

PIZZA PARTY

The Works

ANCHOVIES
MEATBALLS
MUSHROOMS
BROCCOLI
CHEESE
EGGPLANT
GARLIC
BACON
HAM
CLAM

PEPPERONI
SAUSAGE
TOMATO
ONIONS
PEPPERS
SALAMI
SPINACH
SHRIMP
OLIVES
PESTO

```
I L O C C O R B A C O N
M Y S R E P P E P H O U
E G G P L A N T S E S C
A A P E N D E F P E A S
T I M P E S T O I S L M
B N I P I T T V N E A O
A C R E E A O L A Y M O
L I H R M H N M C A I R
L L S O C A I K H E A H
S R T N L O O L I V E S
T A A I O F N D O U G U
E G A S U A S H C L A M
```

Pizza Maze

Dave is constantly delivering pizza to Mr. Gibson's store. How fast can you get the van across town? Find the route that has the least traffic lights. You can travel under the giant pizza slice.

P.S. How many triangular pizza pieces can you find on the way?

What do you like on your pizza? Find all twenty toppings in the grid of letters, above. Then, read the leftover letters from left to right to find out why someone might want to own a pizza shop.

CONSTANTLY PIZZA

28

Extra ZZZ's, Pleeze

Some people like pizza with extra cheese. Here's a bunch of words with double Z's! How many can you figure out?

1. the sound a bee makes   _ _ Z Z
2. type of music   _ _ Z Z
3. to feel like you are spinning   _ _ Z Z _
4. a picture that's not clear   _ _ Z Z _
5. game with interlocking pieces   _ _ Z Z _ _
6. large bird with a bald head   _ _ Z Z _ _ _
7. big snow storm   _ _ _ Z Z _ _ _
8. several short tests   _ _ _ Z Z _ _

29

BOUNCING BABIES

Surprising Seven

Start with the B marked with the black dot. Move clockwise around the puzzle, picking up every third letter. Write the letters on the lines (we have given you the first two). When you are done, you will know who gave birth in 1997 to the first ever thriving set of septuplets.

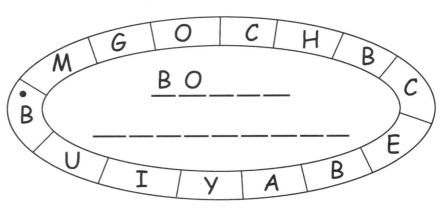

B O _ _ _ _ _

_ _ _ _ _ _ _ _ _

Where Are the Babies?

Drew was reading a story to all the children when Mom left the room. But when Mom returned, all she saw was Drew! Can <u>you</u> find the seven babies? Don't forget to look for their older sister, too.

What Do You Call a Baby?

Draw lines to match the pictures of animal mothers with the names of their babies.
Be careful — several different mamas have babies with the same name.
Other mamas have babies with more than one name!

CALF

KID

FOAL

CUB

LAMB

PIGLET

COLT

FAWN

KIT

PUPPY

DUCKLING

FILLY

Fast 'n' Funny
What did the
baby lightbulb
say to the mama
lightbulb?

I wuv you watts!

31

THE BOOKCASE

Don't Forget About Mervin

Are you still looking for him? He's still hiding somewhere on every two pages.

Book-ish Words

How many of these "book" words do you know?

1. a support at the end
   of a row of books ....BOOK __ __ __

2. a small book or pamphlet ....BOOK __ __ __

3. a set of shelves to hold books ....BOOK __ __ __ __

4. something that holds your
   place in a book ....BOOK __ __ __ __

5. a person who loves to read ....BOOK __ __ __ __

6. owner's label in the
   front of a book ....BOOK __ __ __ __ __

7. a person who keeps
   the records of a business........................BOOK __ __ __ __ __ __

8. a traveling library....................................BOOK __ __ __ __ __ __

9. owner of a book store ....BOOK __ __ __ __ __ __

Reading Rebuses

Need a good read? Solve these rebuses and you'll have an armload of great books to choose from!

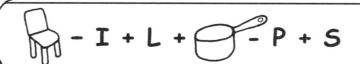

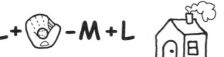

A Good Mystery

Using a simple reversed alphabet code (A = Z, B = Y, C = X, etc.), can you figure out this American proverb?

Z   Y   L   L   P   R   H   Z

__   __ __ __ __   __ __ __

U   I   R   V   M   W

__ __ __ __ __ __

The Book Nook

The answers to these riddles are two single syllable words that rhyme.

1. What do you call someone who steals volumes from the library?

   A _____

2. Where do you hang your wet books to dry?

   On a _____

3. What do you call a chef who boils a dictionary?

   A _____

Oops!

Mervin must be hungry after all his hiding. Use straight lines to finish the letters of the four word book title he just ate.

THE STINKY CHEESE MAN

MUNCH

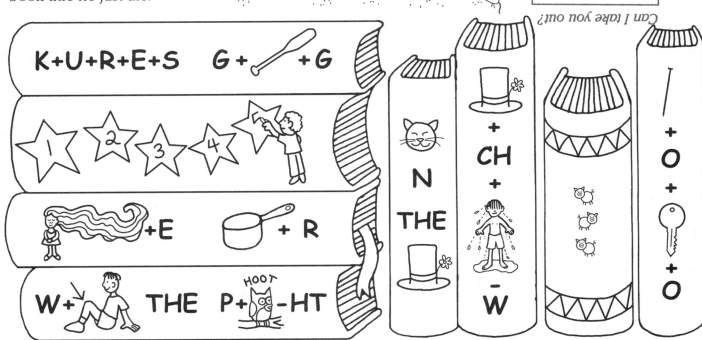

K+U+R+E+S   G+⚾+G

⭐1 ⭐2 ⭐3 ⭐4 ⭐

+E   +R

W+ THE P+HOOT-HT

N THE

+CH+ -W

+O+O+O

TRAVEL USA

License Plate Lottery

Can you name the state from just the slogan on its license plate? We left some U-S-A to help you out!

Across

2. Land of Enchantment
5. First in Flight
7. Famous for Potatoes

Down

1. Wild, Wonderful
2. Live Free or Die
3. 10,000 Lakes
4. Greatest Snow on Earth
6. The Last Frontier

State Scramble

Unscramble each state. After you have written them in the blanks, the shaded letters will spell out the most popular time for travel in the United States.

1. AVEDNA   _ _ _ _ _ _
2. HAIOD   _ _ _ _ _
3. NCTUNTOECIC   _ _ _ _ _ _ _ _ _ _ _
4. GAIVRINI   _ _ _ _ _ _ _ _
5. HOUST TADOAK   _ _ _ _ _ _ _ _ _ _ _
6. ISOULAIAN   _ _ _ _ _ _ _ _ _
7. LINISOIL   _ _ _ _ _ _ _ _
8. WNE CXIOEM   _ _ _ _ _ _ _ _ _

34

Cross-Country Trip

Sonja is driving with her family from your home in Maine back to her house in California. On the way, she stops in eighteen states. At each stop she mails you a postcard with the state abbreviation on it. But the postcards do not arrive in order! See if you can plot Sonja's trip on the map below. Shade in each state as you put the postcards in order from Maine to California.

HIGH TIDE

A Day at the Beach

It's easy to get lost in a crowd. Can you spy where each of these small parts is located
in the big picture? Hint: The small parts might be turned sideways or upside-down!

1.　　　2.　　　3.　　　4.　　　5.　　　6.

Heading Home

Can you get from your vacation at the sea to your home in town? You must travel one space at a time making compound words as you go. You can move up and down, and side to side — but not diagonally!

START			
SEA	SHELL	FISH	HOOK
HORSE	BACK	HAND	BALL
FLY	YARD	OUT	GAME
PAPER	STICK	BREAK	DOWN
BACK	FIRE	FAST	TOWN FINISH

Building Project

Look carefully at the beach scene on the page to the left. Find eleven items that fit into the grid on this page. Each word should read from top to bottom. When you are finished, read across the shaded row of letters to find the name of popular beach houses.

Fast 'n' Funny
Why were there puddles on the beach?

Because the seaweed!

Race to the Finish

These athletes were in a rush to get home! Starting at number 1 and ending at 88, connect the dots to see what they have left on the stadium floor.

Who?

Can you figure out to which well-known athlete each piece of gear belongs? Part of their first name is over part of their last name. Here's a list of possibles:

Tiger Woods
Mark McGwire
Tara Lipinski
Wayne Gretzky
Andre Agassi
Mia Hamm

Michelle Kwan
Bobby Orr
Pete Sampras
Sammy Sousa
Michael Jordan
John Elway

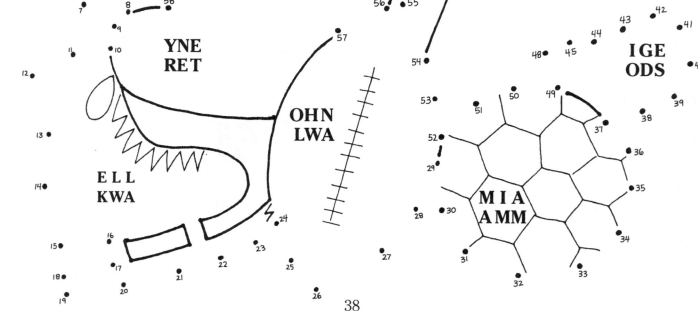

MAR
C GW

PE T
AMP

YNE
RET

ELL
KWA

OHN
LWA

I GE
ODS

MIA
AMM

38

Take Me Out to the Ball Game

See if you can name eleven popular sports that use balls and fit the names into the crisscross grid. We left you some B-O-U-N-C-E and R-O-L-L as hints.

1. _____
2. _____
3. _____
4. _____
5. _____
6. _____
7. _____
8. _____
9. _____
10. _____
11. _____

Fast 'n' Funny
What should a boxer drink before a fight?

Punch!

You Win Some, You Lose Some

Figure out where to put each of the scrambled letters. They all fit in spaces under their own column. When you have filled in the grid, you will be able to read this classic saying about winning and losing.

39

HOT HOBBIES

Cool Collections

Fill in as many collectibles as you can. We left you some D-U-S-T as a hint, since that's what a lot of collections collect!

Across

2. A kind of magazine full of colorful action drawings
4. Soft toys that children cuddle
6. Pieces of metal used as money
8. Hard outer covering of certain animals found at the beach
9. Big paper signs that often have pictures

Down

1. A person's signature, usually someone well known
3. Small circular objects used to fasten clothing
5. Small pieces of paper stuck on letters to show a mailing fee has been paid
7. Toys that look like babies, children, or grown-ups

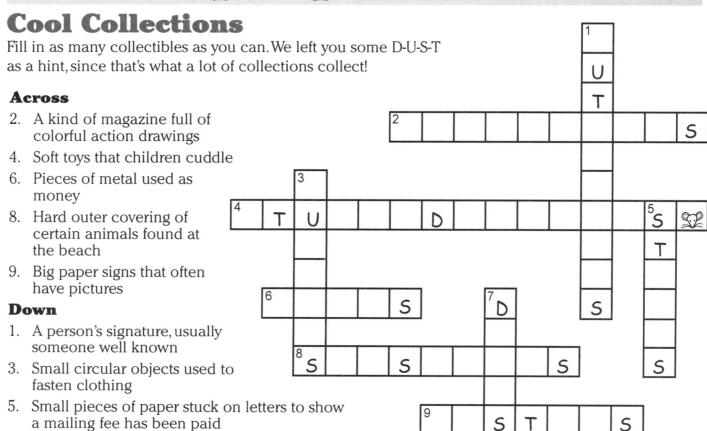

Similar Stamps

Bill loves to collect stamps. But he doesn't want two of the same kind! Can you find the two stamps that are exactly alike and cross out one of them?

40

Build a Model

To construct the model airplane, write the correct part number for each piece on the lines provided. The number shows where each piece belongs in the puzzle grid. We've given you a small picture of the completed airplane to guide you. Caution: Some of the pieces may be upside down!

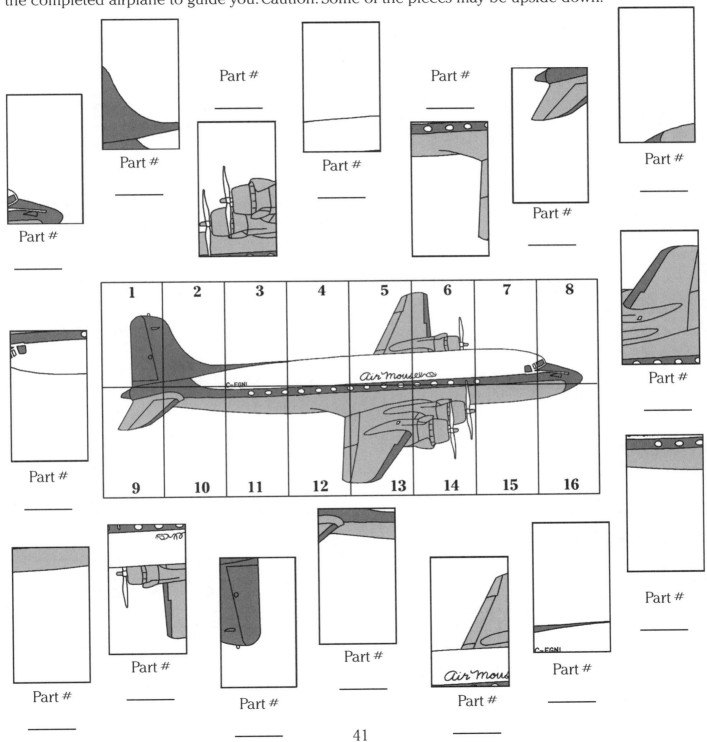

Part #

Part #

Part #

Part #

Part #

Part #

Part #

Part #

Part #

Part #

Part #

Part #

Part #

Part #

Part #

Part #

41

NAME THAT NUMBER

Roman Numerals

People didn't always count 1, 2, 3. They used to count I, II, III, IV!

These are the basic numbers used in the Roman system. The Romans used these seven numbers to make up all their numbers.

I = 1
V = 5
X = 10
L = 50
C = 100
D = 500
M = 1000

Here's how the system works:

If one Roman numeral is followed by a larger one, then the first number is subtracted from the second number.

For example: IX = 10 - 1

But if one Roman numeral is followed by a number that is the same or smaller, you add the numbers together.

For example: VII = 5 + 1 + 1

See if you can write the following in Roman Numerals.

1. Your age: _____

2. The number of minutes in an hour: _____

3. The number of hours in a day: _____

4. The number of days in a year: _____

What's a Googol?

A googol is a REALLY big number. If a ten has one zero (10), how many zeros do you think a googol has? Using a simple number substitution (A=1, B=2, C=3, etc.), see if you can break this number code.

1   7·15·15·7·15·12   8·1·19
__   __ __ __ __ __ __   __ __ __

15·14·5   8·21·14·4·18·5·4
__ __ __   __ __ __ __ __ __ __

26·5·18·15·19
__ __ __ __ __

Hidden Numbers

There is at least one number hidden in each of these sentences. Circle the ones you can find!

1. I love my computer — when it works!

2. Beth reeked of smoke after sitting by the campfire.

3. My mother likes to weigh tomatoes on every scale in the store.

4. Annie was even early for school last week!

5. We can stuff our dirty clothes in your bag.

Quick

Can you turn this number into a mouse?

2

Four Squares

Begin at the white number 4 that is in the dark box. Move up, down, or sideways four spaces in any direction. Add the numbers as you go and reach all four corners, but only one time each. What path must you take to have the sum of all the numbers you land on add up to 46? Hint: The pattern forms the outline of a letter of the alphabet.

```
4 2 4 3 1 3 4 2 4
2 1 2 4 3 4 2 1 2
1 2 4 3 2 3 4 2 3
3 4 3 2 1 2 3 4 1
4 3 2 1 4 1 2 1 2
3 4 3 2 1 2 3 4 1
1 2 4 3 2 3 4 2 3
2 1 2 4 1 4 2 1 2
4 2 4 1 3 1 4 2 4
```

Cross Sums

You must figure out what combination of numbers to use so that each column or row adds up to the totals shown in the white numbers. The white arrows show you in which direction you will be adding, and we have left you some numbers as hints. Better sharpen your pencil!

Here are a few simple rules:

— You are only adding the numbers in any set of white boxes that are touching each other.

— Use only the numbers 1 through 9. Each number can only be used once in each set.

Remember, you need to think ahead a little bit. Each number has to be correct both across and down!

43

Travel Back in Time

Can you place the following inventions on the time line in the correct order in which they were invented?

Bicycle

X-Ray

Paper

Telephone

Sewing Machine

Windshield Wipers

Microwave Oven

Helicopter

Zipper

Parachute

White Out!

Bette Nesmith Graham invented a very functional fluid! It is something which makes life much easier for people who need to correct mistakes. Turn to each page listed below and find the "white" letter. Fill these letters into their proper square. When you are finished, you will have the name of her invention.

Page 4

Page 6

Page 9

Page 11

Page 21

Page 37

Page 45

Page 54

Page 79

Page 97

Page 114

Fast 'n' Funny

What did the inventor get when he crossed a turkey with an octopus?

Enough drumsticks for everyone at dinner!

AD105   1785   1846   1876   1885

Why Didn't I Think of That?

Can you guess each of these famous inventions? Write your guess in each box.

1.

I'm an invention that your mom, dad, or other adult probably reminds you to use every night before you go to bed. What am I?

2.

I come in fun flavors and am perfect to lick on a hot day. What am I?

3.

I'm such a talented invention that I can sleep, walk the dog, and shoot the moon! What am I?

4.

I'm a good writer, but not an author. I leave blue or black lines on white sheets, but not in a bed. I have a ball in my point, but don't bounce! What am I?

Fast 'n' Famous

Thomas Alva Edison, inventor of the lightbulb, phonograph, movie projector, and over 1,000 other patented inventions, said "To invent, you need a good imagination and a pile of junk."

5.

I'm a mixed-up invention — in a car accident, I explode to keep you safe! What am I?

6.

I'm an invention that gets right to the heart of the matter. I love listening to a good beat. What am I?

7.

I can get rid of your headache or bring down your fever, but I'm not a doctor. What am I?

8.

I have more memory than an elephant, but you can lift me with one hand. What am I?

9.

I was invented by someone who was impressed by the way certain prickly plants stick to your clothes. What am I?

1891   1895   1903   1939   1947

SIGNS & SYMBOLS

Shape-ly Squares

Use the following six shapes to fill in the holes in the grid: circle, star, diamond, square, hexagon, triangle. The object is to have each shape appear only ONCE in each row or column.

Fast Signs

Can you guess what these symbols stand for?

_____

_____

_____

It's Symbolic!

Crack this code to find a tongue twister about symbols. Some of the letters have been provided to help you get started. Write your answers on the lines under the code.

A = !   > = V
S = $ (= I
L = #   B = +

$! # # ‹ $! &
— — — — —   — — —

$ = > = @ ! # $ (# # ‹
— — — — — — —   — — — —

$ ‹) + % # $ Ɛ :›
— — — — — — —   — — —

46

Stop & Go

Lulu wants to bring her friend Larry some library books while he is in the hospital. Use the key provided to locate the library and the hospital. Then, mark Lulu's route from the library's closest parking lot to the hospital's closest parking lot. A <u>STOP</u> or <u>NO ENTRY</u> sign means you may not go that way. A <u>ONE WAY</u> sign means you can only go the way the arrow is pointing.

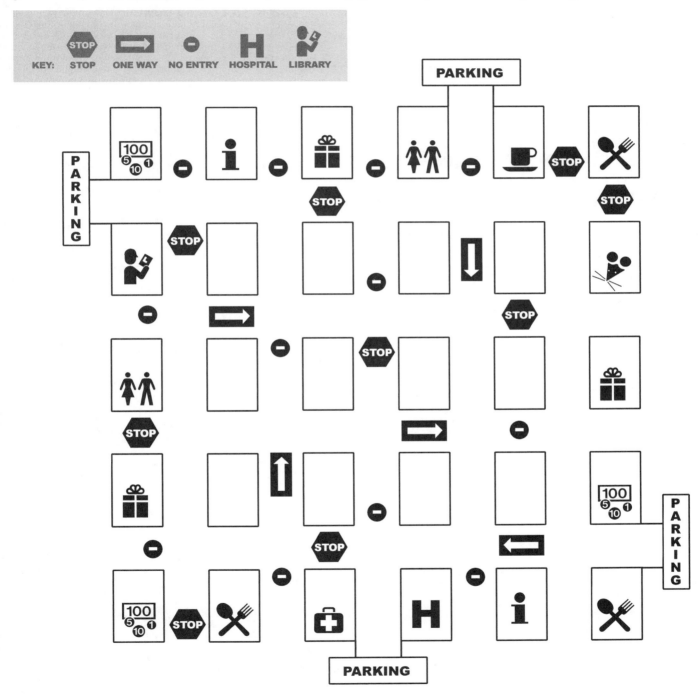

WACKY WORD PLAY

Idiotic Idioms

An idiom is a phrase that cannot be understood from the meanings of the separate words in it. Look at the pictures and see if you can guess the expressions for the following meanings.

1. All at once

_ _ _ _

_ _ _ _ _ _

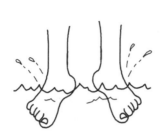

2. Try something new

_ _ _   _ _ _ _

_ _ _ _   _ _ _ _

3. To study

_ _ _   _ _ _ _   _ _ _ _ _

4. On top of things

_ _   _ _ _

_ _ _ _

5. Undecided

_ _   _ _ _

_ _ _ _ _

6. Tell a secret

_ _ _   _ _ _   _ _ _   _ _ _

_ _   _ _ _   _ _ _

7. Get some sleep

_ _ _ _ _   _ _ _ _   _ ' _

48

Hink Pinks

The answers to Hink Pinks are two rhyming words of one syllable each. We did the first one for you!

1. happy boy .... G L A D   L A D
2. not real reptile .... _ _ _ _   _ _ _ _ _
3. splendid group
   of musicians .... _ _ _ _ _   _ _ _ _
4. a group yell .... _ _ _ _   _ _ _ _ _ _
5. a skinny female ruler .... _ _ _ _   _ _ _ _ _
6. a large branch .... _ _ _   _ _ _ _
7. a cold swimming place .... _ _ _ _   _ _ _ _
8. a drink at noon .... _ _ _ _ _   _ _ _ _ _
9. a made smaller
   black & white animal .... _ _ _ _ _ _   _ _ _ _ _
10. a ditch in Paris .... _ _ _ _ _ _   _ _ _ _ _ _

Onomatopoeia

Onomatopoeia simply means a word that sounds like its meaning, for example <u>click</u> or <u>hum</u>. Look at the pictures below and see if you can find their sounds in the letter grid.

```
S D H O N K U V P
J L R G W R E L Z
H S U I U J U Z R
B I P R P G U E E
L K S L P B P V V
A Y Q S A S P G M
Z K U O I S C O Z
I H O H Z I H B P
P M W I F M E O W
```

49

WACKIER WORD PLAY

Dictionary Dissection

How many words can you make out of the word DICTIONARY? See if you can make fifty-two!

1. _____
2. _____
3. _____
4. _____
5. _____
6. _____
7. _____
8. _____
9. _____
10. _____
11. _____
12. _____
13. _____

14. _____
15. _____
16. _____
17. _____
18. _____
19. _____
20. _____
21. _____
22. _____
23. _____
24. _____
25. _____
26. _____

27. _____
28. _____
29. _____
30. _____
31. _____
32. _____
33. _____
34. _____
35. _____
36. _____
37. _____
38. _____
39. _____

40. _____
41. _____
42. _____
43. _____
44. _____
45. _____
46. _____
47. _____
48. _____
49. _____
50. _____
51. _____
52. _____

Alliteration

Saying series of similar sounds — that's alliteration! The five pictures to the right each represent a phrase where all the words start with the same sound. Can you guess each phrase?

CL_____

CL_____

SH_____

SH_____

50

Simply Synonyms

Synonyms are words that have the same, or almost the same, meaning. We have chosen four synonyms for each word listed below. How quickly can you find them in the word list and write them where they belong?

Fast 'n' Funny

Which word is always pronounced wrong?

Wrong!

LITTLE = _____   _____   _____   _____

WALK = _____   _____   _____   _____

FUNNY = _____   _____   _____   _____

POKE = _____   _____   _____   _____

GROUP = _____   _____   _____   _____

STAY = _____   _____   _____   _____

BEND = _____   _____   _____   _____

WORD LIST

JAB	WEIRD	SMALL	BATCH	TWIST	STROLL	CURIOUS
STEP	WAIT	PROD	TURN	LINGER	CLUSTER	HIKE
STOP	TINY	CROWD	REMAIN	PLOD	SKIMPY	BUNCH
ODD	STAB	WIND	SLIGHT	STICK	CURVE	STRANGE

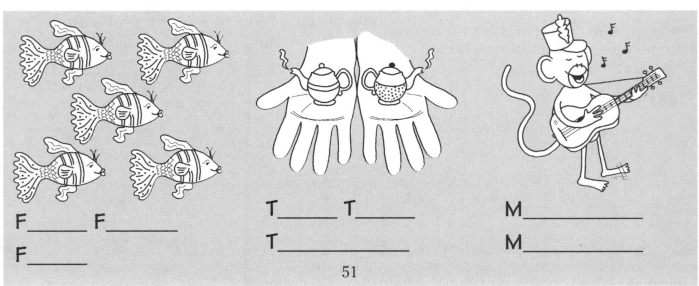

F_____ F_____
F_____

T_____ T_____
T_____

M_____
M_____

51

WACKIEST WORD PLAY EVER!

Blended Words

Many words are a combinaton of two words.
Can you unscramble the following blended words?

1. breakfast + lunch = NUBHRC

2. flutter + hurry = RYULFR

3. motor + hotel = LEMOT

4. smack + mash = SHAMS

5. smoke + fog = OGMS

6. squirm + wiggle = QUEGIGSL

7. twist + whirl = WLRIT

8. chuckle + snort = HELTROC

Fast 'n' Funny

What time is the same whether it goes backward or forward?

Noon!

What word begins with E, ends with E, and sounds as if it has only one letter in it?

Eye!

Perfect Palindromes

A palindrome is a word or sentence that reads the same both forward and backward. Can you figure out the missing letters in each of these palindromes?

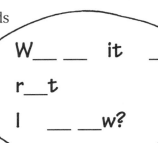

W__ __ it __
r__t
l __ __w?

1. W__   s__w

2. __ur__e__   ru__

3. __te__   o__   __o   __et__

4. __e__er   o__ __   or   e__e__

52

Short n' Sweet

Acronyms are abbreviations formed from the first letters or other parts of a group of words. See if you can guess what each acronym stands for by looking at the pictures. Write your answer on the lines.

Today's special is a tomato sandwich.
Put bacon and lettuce on mine.

B _____
L _____
T _____

This looks like a quiet spot.
R.I.P.

R _____
I _____
P _____

HELP!
HELP!

S _____
O _____
S _____

SMOOCH!

S _____
W _____
A _____
K _____

I had a bad day at school, Dad.
Here's your teddy, honey.

T _____
L _____
C _____

Everyone's been waiting for him to arrive!

V _____
I _____
P _____

What is it?
I don't know, but it's moving fast!

U _____
F _____
O _____

OK fans, now for my favorite record...

D _____
J _____

Hey, this is <u>my</u> work!

M _____
Y _____
O _____
B _____

HURRY! Mail this right away!
Don't wait!

A _____
S _____
A _____
P _____

THINGS TO DO
ASAP ... NOW!
I sure am glad it's the end of the week!
TO DO

T _____
G _____
I _____
F _____

S _____
C _____
U _____
B _____
A _____

53

USE IT AGAIN, SAM

Recycled Words

See if you can turn the first word into the last word by changing ONE letter at a time to make the next new word in line.

1. PIG - _____ - _____ - LEG

2. FOOD - _____ - _____ - COOK

3. HAND - _____ - _____ - SEED

4. CAN - _____ - _____ - _____ - BET

5. JUNK - _____ - _____ - _____ - BANK

Fast 'n' Funny
What has four wheels and flies?

A garbage truck!

Don't Throw It Out!

Hey, there's lots of good junk in this pile! Can you find five things that don't have to go to the dump, but could be recycled or reused?

1. _____
2. _____
3. _____
4. _____
5. _____

Can you also find three things that could be hazardous and should definitely <u>not</u> be just dumped?

1. _____

2. _____

3. _____

New Life for an Old Joke

To solve this puzzle, figure out where to put each of the scrambled letters. They all fit in spaces under their own column. When you have correctly filled in the grid, you will have the answer to this riddle:

Why are garbage collectors sometimes sad?

	E	E		U	F	E		N		M	O			
B	R	N		O	H	T		D	U	D	P	W	
A	I	C	A	T	S	E	E	T	H	E	Y	S	N

Back to Nature

Figure out the mystery words from the clues. Then read the circled letters to discover what you get when you mix all of these things together in a pile out in the yard. We left you some W-O-R-M-S as a hint, because they <u>love</u> this stuff (and they're good for it, too)!

1. Left over after a dark brown breakfast drink is brewed.

   (◯)o _ _ _ _   _ ro _ _ _ s

2. What is left after you burn logs in the fireplace.

   w (◯)o _   _ s _ _ _ _

3. Waste matter from farm animals.

   (m) _ _ _ _ r _

4. The vegetable skins that are removed before cooking.

   (◯) _ _ _ s

5. These creatures are good for the soil.

   w (o) r m s

6. These fall off trees in the fall.

   _ _ _ _ _ (◯)

7. Apples, bananas, cherries, etc.

   _ r _ (◯)

   Mystery Word _ _ _ _ _ _ _ _

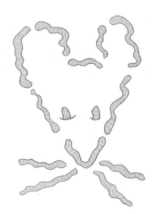

55

Kriss Kross

Don't be bored — see if you can get all ten of
these board games into their proper place!

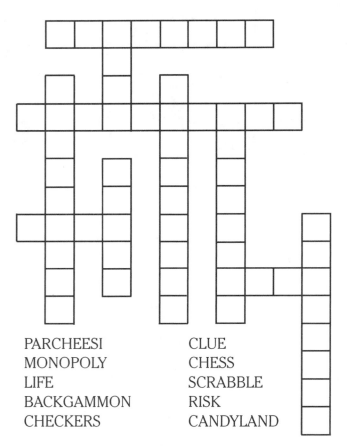

PARCHEESI   CLUE

MONOPOLY   CHESS

LIFE   SCRABBLE

BACKGAMMON   RISK

CHECKERS   CANDYLAND

Disappearing Dots

Dylan has Dominoes with disappearing dots!
Can you replace the correct number of dots
(one through six) on each disturbed domino?

Hopscotch Addition

Bet you've never played hopscotch this
way! Use the numbered hopscotch board
below and for each "turn" add up the
numbers in the spaces on which you
hop.

For example, on your
first turn you would
"hop" over number
one, so don't count
it. As you keep hop-
ping up the board,
add 2+3+4+5+6+7
+8+9+10. Turn
around and hop
back down the
board adding 9+8+7
+6+5+4+3+2 for a total
of 98 points.

On your second turn
you would hop on
1, hop over 2 (so
don't count it), and keep
on going.

QUESTION: How many
turns would it take to get
380 points?

How Many Marbles?

Sandy, Peter, and Flo are playing marbles. To find out how many marbles each child has, add the numbers that make a straight line through the circle from where each player shoots.

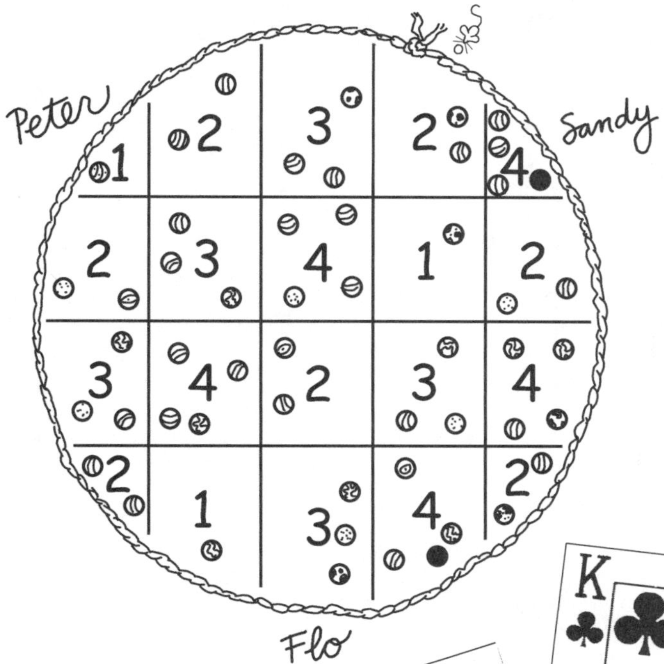

Peter

Sandy

Flo

Jumble of Jacks

Find your way from the first jack to the ball.

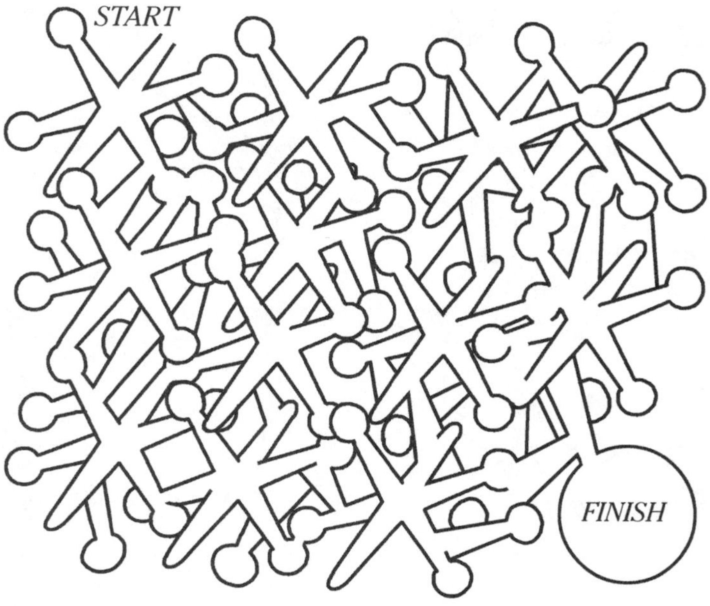

START

FINISH

Two of a Kind

You are holding a handful of Kings, and two of them are exactly the same. Which two are they?

57

A CAMPING WE WILL GO

In the Wild

Ryan's family packed in a hurry for their camping trip. Take a good look at the picture of their campsite, right. Can you see what fourteen items they brought by mistake?

Triangle Teaser

Color in each three-sided shape to find out where your dog sleeps when he goes camping with you.

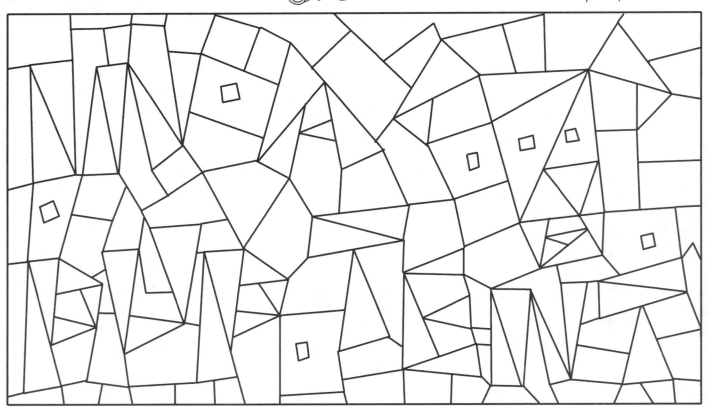

Midnight Morse Message

Late at night Ryan sends his brother Danny this secret message using his flashlight. But you know Morse code, too, so you can tell what the two of them are planning to do. Hint: The slash mark (/) in the message is the space between letters.

A •—   E •   O ———   T —   , ——••——

C —•—•   H ••••   R •—•   W •——   ? ••——••

D —••   N —•   S •••   Y —•——

—•• / •— / —• / —•• / —•——   ——••——

•—— / •— / —• / —   —• / ———

••• / —•—• / •—• / —•• / •   — / •••• / •

——— / — / •••• / — / •—• / — / •••   ••——••

•—• / —•—— / •— / —•

59

FEELING FUNNY

Sad Man/ Glad Man

Sometimes you're happy. Sometimes you're not. Can you help Sad Man move through the maze so he is happy at the end? Make a path that alternates sad man (☹) and glad man (☺). You can move up and down, or side-to-side, but not diagonally. If you hit a mad man (😐), you are going in the wrong direction!

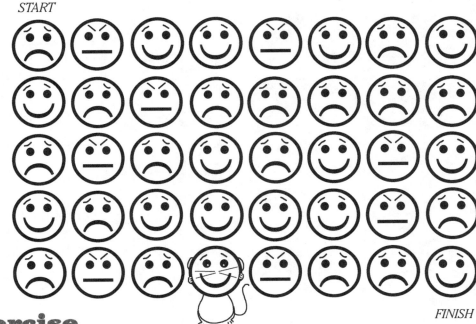

START

FINISH

Emotional Exercise

How many words can you find in the word EMOTIONAL? Bet you can find over fifty!

1. _____	14. _____	27. _____	40. _____
2. _____	15. _____	28. _____	41. _____
3. _____	16. _____	29. _____	42. _____
4. _____	17. _____	30. _____	43. _____
5. _____	18. _____	31. _____	44. _____
6. _____	19. _____	32. _____	45. _____
7. _____	20. _____	33. _____	46. _____
8. _____	21. _____	34. _____	47. _____
9. _____	22. _____	35. _____	48. _____
10. _____	23. _____	36. _____	49. _____
11. _____	24. _____	37. _____	50. _____
12. _____	25. _____	38. _____	51. _____
13. _____	26. _____	39. _____	52. _____

Quotable Quote

Answer as many clues as you can, and fill the letters you have into the grid. Work back and forth between the quotation box and clues until you can read what former First Lady Eleanor Roosevelt had to say about feelings.

1	2		3	4	5		6	7	8		9	10	11	12		13	14	15
	16	17	18	19		20	21	22	23	24	25	26	27		28	29	30	31
32	33	34		35	36	37	38		39	40	41	42	43	44	45			

A. Sing without words = $\frac{}{31}\ \frac{}{33}\ \frac{}{9}$

B. Seven days = $\frac{}{28}\ \frac{}{5}\ \frac{}{18}\ \frac{}{11}$

C. To touch = $\frac{}{16}\ \frac{}{3}\ \frac{}{12}\ \frac{}{19}$

D. Not me = $\frac{}{35}\ \frac{}{3}\ \frac{}{37}$

E. In a little while = $\frac{}{42}\ \frac{}{14}\ \frac{}{36}\ \frac{}{2}$

F. Midday = $\frac{}{4}\ \frac{}{40}\ \frac{}{32}\ \frac{}{44}$

G. Not skinny = $\frac{}{22}\ \frac{}{7}\ \frac{}{30}$

H. Larger than a town = $\frac{}{39}\ \frac{}{25}\ \frac{}{34}\ \frac{}{13}$

I. Faster than a walk = $\frac{}{24}\ \frac{}{15}\ \frac{}{1}$

J. More pleasant = $\frac{}{41}\ \frac{}{20}\ \frac{}{6}\ \frac{}{43}\ \frac{}{38}$

K. Not far = $\frac{}{41}\ \frac{}{17}\ \frac{}{10}\ \frac{}{27}$

L. Toward the inside = $\frac{}{29}\ \frac{}{8}\ \frac{}{45}\ \frac{}{26}$

How Do You Feel?

Look at the picture below. Try and guess the phrase that means you are VERY happy.

" _ _   _ _ _ _ _   _ _ _ _ "

Love to Laugh

Laugh out loud or quietly to yourself — can you fill in five different kinds of laughs? We gave you a couple of L-A-U-G-Hs to get you started.

FAMILY REUNION

The Newlywed Name

Some people combine their last names when they get married. See if you can make some familiar compound words by matching up these couples. Write their new married name on the lines below.

Katie

Franny

Paula

Julie

Rita

Tammy

Nathan

Frank

Brian

Peter

Steven

Chris

1. Mrs. Katie _____

2. Mrs. Franny _____

3. Mrs. Paula_____

4. Mrs. Julie _____

5. Mrs. Rita _____

6. Mrs. Tammy _____

Oh, Brother!

Jennifer comes from a large family. How many brothers and sisters do you think she has? Find out by crossing out the following names from the grid, below.

1. Cross out all the names that start with the letter S.

2. Cross out all the names that end with the letter N.

3. Cross out all the names that start and end with the same letter.

Sara	Allan	Bob	Billy
David	Sylvia	Kathy	Elise
Ryan	Simon	Anna	Kevin
Sonja	Philip	Sandy	Georg
Tom	Therese	John	Ian
Otto	Sharon	Mervin	Fran
Brian	Seth	Mary	Lynn
Sam	Nan	Robin	Erin
Susan	Karen	Steven	Jim

Jennifer has _____ brothers and _____ sisters.

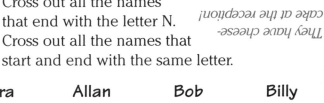

A Flurry of Families

A family is a group, but not all groups are called families. Unscramble the letters to find which kind of animal lives in what kind of group.

1. IHSF _____live in a SCHOOL

2. SNILO _____live in a PRIDE

3. XEON_____live in a YOKE

4. ESBE _____live in a SWARM

5. EHPSE _____live in a FLOCK

6. SANT _____live in a COLONY

7. EEESG _____live in a GAGGLE

8. DKSCU _____live in a BRACE

9. SODG _____live in a PACK

10. IHSKCC_____live in a CLUTCH

11. VESDO _____live in a COVEY

12. EMOSKNY _____live in a TROOP

13. SAMCL _____live in a BED

14. TBAIBRS _____live in a DOWN

15. ANSWS_____live in a BEVY

16. SEHALW _____live in a POD

63

Parents and children may not look exactly alike, but often people can pick family members out of a group. Study the following faces and see if you can do it, too. Draw a line matching each pair of relatives.

BEST FRIENDS

Quotable Quote

Answer as many clues as you can, and fill the letters you have into the grid. Work back and forth between the quotation box and clues until you can read what writer and poet Ralph Waldo Emerson had to say about being a friend.

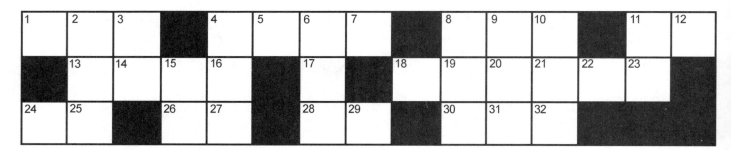

A. One more than four
$\overline{18}\ \overline{24}\ \overline{15}\ \overline{3}$

B. Person between the ages of 13 - 19
$\overline{1}\ \overline{29}\ \overline{21}\ \overline{31}$

C. Noise an owl makes
$\overline{13}\ \overline{27}\ \overline{30}\ \overline{11}$

D. To show the way
$\overline{6}\ \overline{32}\ \overline{9}\ \overline{23}$

E. To melt
$\overline{26}\ \overline{2}\ \overline{17}\ \overline{8}$

F. Not a girl
$\overline{28}\ \overline{12}\ \overline{7}$

G. Cats like to play with a ball of this
$\overline{10}\ \overline{14}\ \overline{19}\ \overline{5}$

H. A loud sound
$\overline{22}\ \overline{4}\ \overline{20}\ \overline{25}\ \overline{16}$

One Scoop — Or Two?

Joey, Mark, and Aaron want to buy ice cream. They empty their pockets to see how much money they have.

Joey = $1.15

Mark = $1.78

Aaron = $1.42

A single-scoop cone costs $1.25 and a double-scoop cone costs $1.50. If the boys pool all their money, do they have enough to each get double scoops?

Share & Share Alike

Andrew, Jay, and Josh are friends who share everything. Today they went apple picking and came home with thirteen apples. Some of the apples are really big, and some are pretty tiny. How can the three boys divide the apples evenly if they don't have a scale with which to weigh them?

Stephanie's Sleepover

Stephanie had a gigantic sleepover party — there were 15 kids all together! The girls were being silly and arranged their sleeping bags to look like the following impossible math equation:

However, four of the guests had to go home early. After they left, Stephanie noticed that the math equation now worked! Can you figure out which four bags were taken away? Color in the remaining bags to see the numbers clearly.

• •

Nice Neighbors

Nina, Lauren, Blair, and Dylan all live in the same neighborhood. Using the clues, can you decide in which house each child lives?

* Nina lives on Pine Street.

* Dylan lives diagonally across the street from Blair.

* Lauren lives down the street from Nina, but on the opposite side.

* Blair lives across the street from Nina.

* Lauren and Dylan live in the same block, but not on the same street.

* Blair does not live on Pine Street.

* Nina must cross Pine Street to visit Blair or Dylan.

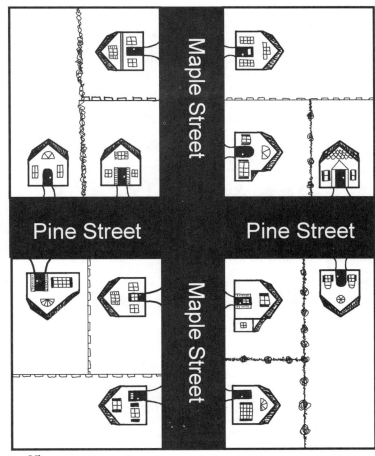

HOME SWEET HOME

Household Words

There are lots of compound words that begin with the word "house." How many can you figure out?

1. A grayish winged bug that eats garbage .... H O U S E _ _ _

2. A floating vessel that people live on .... H O U S E _ _ _ _

3. All the people who live in a home .... H O U S E _ _ _ _

4. Cleaning, cooking, etc. .... H O U S E _ _ _ _

5. It is green and is grown indoors .... H O U S E _ _ _ _ _

6. A person who is paid to take care of a large household .... H O U S E _ _ _ _ _ _

At Home Wherever They Go

Unscramble the names of these four creatures that carry their homes with them on their backs.

1. LAINS _____

2. MERITH BRAC_____

3. LETRUT_____

4. KPARABCKCE _____

A House for Me

Draw a line to match each character with their home.

Habitat Is Where It's At

There are many different places where animals live. Each has its own climate and types of plants. Think of six different habitats that can be found around the world and fit them into the grid, below. The numbered clues are a big hint — they show you one animal from each of the regions!

ACROSS

2. "There is a lot of tall, skinny stuff all over the ground in my habitat."

4. "My habitat can get VERY cold and dark for six months of the year."

6. "If you come to my habitat, you'd better bring an umbrella!"

DOWN

1. "Most people would need ropes and special boots to climb all the way up to my habitat."

3. "My habitat is full of sand. Better bring some water to drink!"

5. "It's a long swim to land from my habitat."

Can You Speak the Language?

Using a computer requires its own sort of language. Do a search for all twenty-four of the computer terms listed below in the grid.

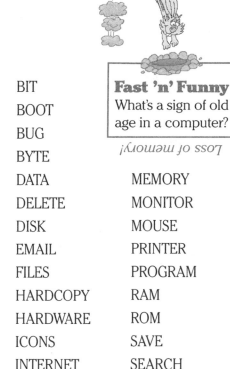

```
Y  L  D  E  L  E  T  E  B  K  P  Y
F  D  Y  I  C  O  N  S  U  X  R  P
I  C  A  N  K  S  I  D  G  O  O  O
L  M  B  T  H  O  S  D  M  I  G  C
E  O  N  E  A  F  R  E  D  S  R  D
S  N  E  R  R  T  M  N  A  E  A  R
R  I  S  N  D  W  G  V  T  R  M  A
N  T  U  E  W  A  E  Y  Q  A  C  H
B  O  O  T  A  R  B  S  A  M  D  H
I  R  M  O  R  E  T  N  I  R  P  S
T  C  L  K  E  Y  B  O  A  R  D  U
```

Fast 'n' Funny
What's a sign of old age in a computer?

¡ʎɹoɯǝɯ ɟo sso˥

BIT	
BOOT	
BUG	
BYTE	
DATA	MEMORY
DELETE	MONITOR
DISK	MOUSE
EMAIL	PRINTER
FILES	PROGRAM
HARDCOPY	RAM
HARDWARE	ROM
ICONS	SAVE
INTERNET	SEARCH
KEYBOARD	SOFTWARE

Keyboard Code

An English mathematician named Charles Babbage was the first person to figure out how a machine could perform calculations and store the results. Crack this keyboard code to find out his nickname.

5Y3

RQ5Y34

9R

D9J07534W

Dumb Deletions

Doug e-mailed Dave some of his favorite tongue twisters, but he accidentally kept hitting the delete key. Can you figure out what each phrase was supposed to say?

1. V __ __ tual

   Vir __ __

2. D__ __ ble

   D __ ta

3. Pe__ __ __ ct

   Pa __ __ __ ord

Micro Maze

Can you get Tanya's e-mail through the Internet to her Aunt Mia? Follow the black line from computer to computer. Don't stop for any on-line shopping!

Smiley E-Mail

Smilies are little pictures you can type on your computer using punctuation marks, numbers, and letters. Tilt your head to the left to correctly see the smilies. For example, the original smiley looks like this :-) . Can you see the smiling face? Now, finish the following e-mail letter using only five of the smilies provided.

Possible Smilies

> :)	: - D
: - *	: - o
: - c	; -)
: - I I	: X<

_____! My _____ ate
Uh oh!   cat

something _____
                 sour

and is very _____.
            unhappy

What a little _____
              devil

he is!

SCHOOL DAZE

```
J I H Z O R B S J S
K A P E N C I L P N
J R C J F O N S O A
B O O K S E D T S C
M Y Y W E W E D R K
O G M P E T R R E R
N T S A M M U G K U
E P E P P D O L R L
Y E K E S U O H A E
M N E R A S E R M R
```

It's in My Backpack... Somewhere!

Hidden in the puzzle, left, are fifteen items that are often stuffed in a backpack. As you search through the letter grid, circle each item you find. The words can run forward, backward, up and down, or diagonally.

Subject Scramble

Each scrambled word is a subject you take in school. Unscramble them all, then read the circled letters from top to bottom. They will spell out many student's favorite period of the day!

1. DIGNERA .... ◯ __ __ __ __ __ __

2. CENCIES .... __ ◯ __ __ __ __ __

3. HATSEMICAMT .... __ __ __ __ __ __ __ __ __ ◯ __

4. DESHYP .... __ __ __ __ . ◯ __ .

5. LIOCAS DUTESIS ...... ◯ __ __ __ __ __ __
   ◯ __ __ __ __ __ __ __

   MYSTERY WORD __ __ __ __ __ __

70

Fast 'n' Funny
How many books can you put in an empty backpack?

One, because then it is not empty!

Whose Is Whose?

Laura is looking for her Math book. Unfortunately, the whole class has the same book and parts of each kid's name have rubbed off. Can you figure out which book is Laura's? See if you can figure out the names of her classmates, too.

Hot Lunch

Ryan's mom gave him $2.00 for lunch. If he buys an apple and a cookie, what hot lunch item and drink will he have to get?

MENU
Pizza $1.00
Hot Dog $1.25
Cheeseburger $1.50

Milk $.50	Cookie $.50
Juice $.75	Chips $.50
Water Free	Fruit $.50

Bus Stop

John can't remember the number of his school bus, but he does remember that his bus is different from all the others. Can you tell which bus John should take?

71

AROUND THE WORLD

Stars & Stripes

These three flags are very similar to each other. But each country uses a different symbol in the upper left-hand corner. Can you break the code that tells you which symbol goes on which flag? When you have, complete each flag by drawing in the proper symbol.

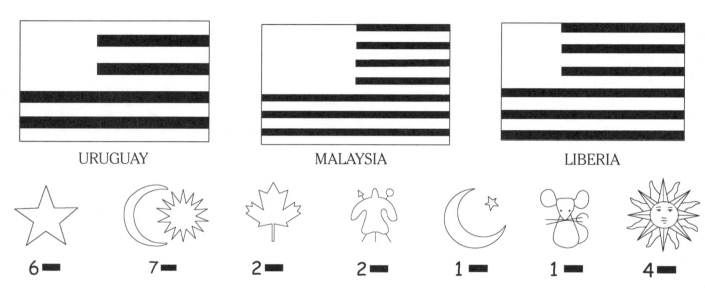

URUGUAY   MALAYSIA   LIBERIA

6 ▬   7 ▬   2 ▬   2 ▬   1 ▬   1 ▬   4 ▬

Hello Friend

You have just gotten a letter from your new pen pal, but he wrote it in Portuguese! Use the dictionary below to read his letter.

Dictionary

amigo	friend	meu	my
anos	years	moro	live
contar	to sing	na	in
dez	ten	nome	name
e	and	novo	new
é	is	Oi!	Hi!
escrever	to write	por favor	please
você escreve	you write	que	what
fazer	to do	seu	your
gostar	to like	ter	to have
eu gosto	I like	eu tenho	I have
você gosto	you like	tocar	to play music
logo	soon	violão	guitar
morar	to live	você	you

Oi!

Meu nome é Rodolfo. Eu tenho dez anos e moro na Brazil. Eu gosto de contar e tocar violão. E você, o que gosta de fazer? Por favor me escreve logo!

seu novo amigo, Rodolfo

World Wide Word Search

There are 192 countries in the world. Can you find the 55 countries represented here in the grid? Answers can go left to right, top to bottom and diagonally. Once you're done, read the leftover letters from left to right and top to bottom find out which country has the largest population.

Angola
Argentina
Australia
Brazil
Bulgaria
Canada
Chile
Colombia
Cuba
Denmark
Egypt
Ethiopia
Fiji
Finland
France
Germany
Great Britain
Greece
Hungary
India
Indonesia
Iran
Iraq
Italy
Japan
Kazakhstan
Libya
Liberia
Malaysia

Mexico
Mongolia
New Zealand
Norway
Oman
Pakistan
Peru
Philippines
Poland
Qatar
Romania
Russia
Saudi Arabia
South Africa
Spain
Sweden
Thailand
Turkey
Ukraine
United States
Uruguay
Venezuela
Vietnam
Yugoslavia
Zimbabwe

```
C P H I E M F O M A N T U R K E Y A Y D A
I N H N N T O R A H A I N D I A D R N L A
V S E I T D H N A Q A T A R H A A A E I A
E I L W L A O I G N P E R U N G L U L I R
S P E L Z I G N O O C E S A N N Z A B S A
S W O T I E P G E P L E C U I E R M E L I
A S E L N B A P R S I I H F N T O T O T R
U O P D A A E L I E I A A E S L A G C O A
D U P U E N M R A N A A V U O T N L U A N
I T L I T N D A I N E T A C S A I O B J N
A H I R O F I E T A D S B D D B H E A A E
R A B A O S C N E H A N E R G E R U N P G
A F Y Q S E A E D I A T A B I E N A R A Y
B R A U E I W A V T I N T R U T R M Z N P
I I R R N B I A S N A Y U H G L A M A I T
A C G A A S L H U T A Y M K A E G I A R L
E A M B Y S K D S U A & N E R I N A N N K
I O M A O A N I G W E T Y T X A L T R W Y
R I L G Z O K U R X S P A I N I I A I I N
Z A U A A A R O I T A L Y T I O C N N N A
M Y K N P U N C H I L E F I J I S O E D A
```

Home Away from Home

Figure out where to put each of the scrambled letters. They all fit in spaces under their own column. When you fill in the grid, you will have a Danish proverb about languages.

H	A		G		E		E		I	S				T		
H	O	M	W	H	A	V	K	N	O	W	H	E	R		H	
L	E	N	E	U	O	G	E	R	Y	W	S	A	T	E	E	

73

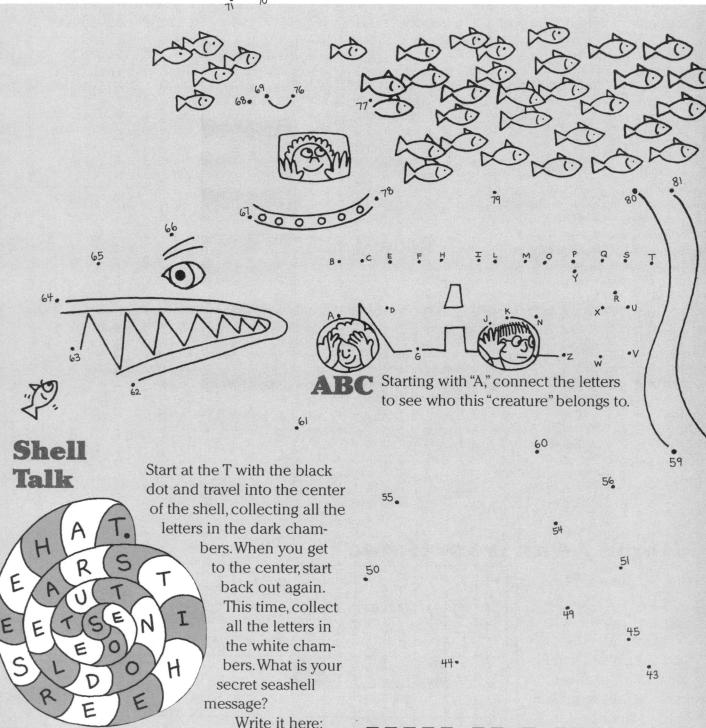

ABC Starting with "A," connect the letters to see who this "creature" belongs to.

Shell Talk

Start at the T with the black dot and travel into the center of the shell, collecting all the letters in the dark chambers. When you get to the center, start back out again. This time, collect all the letters in the white chambers. What is your secret seashell message?

Write it here: _ _ _ _ _ _ _ _ _ _ _ _ _

School of Fish

Fish traveling in groups called schools move so fast that they are hard to count! First, guess how many fish are in this school. Then, circle them in groups of five. Catching them this way makes counting easier.

Your Guess	Exact Number

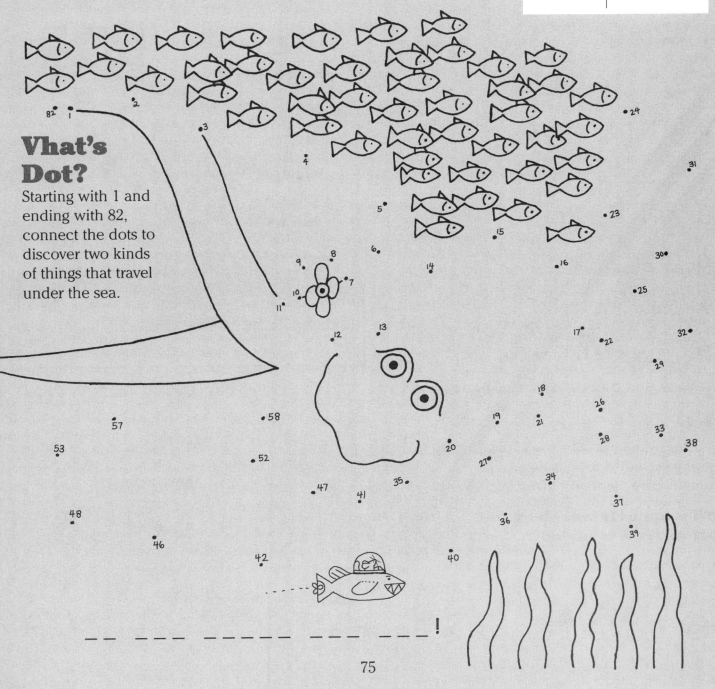

Vhat's Dot?

Starting with 1 and ending with 82, connect the dots to discover two kinds of things that travel under the sea.

75

Missing Parts

Part of each of these words has magically disappeared. Can you find the missing section of each word in the column of word parts on the right?

1. W I Z _ _ _

2. _ _ _ G H T

3. U N I _ _ _ N

4. T _ _ _ L

5. F A I _ _ _ S

6. _ _ _ M E

7. D R _ _ _ N

8. _ _ _ N C E S S

Missing Parts
AGO
COR
GNO
RIE
ROL
PRI
KNI
ARD

A Corner Castle

Can you count how many squares and rectangles it takes to make this castle?

Elf Talk

Use the decoder at right to read the message below. When you're finished, you will have the answer to this riddle:

Why can only two elves sit under a toadstool?

Help!

Connect the dots quickly to find out the helpful answer to this riddle:

What time is it when a princess gets captured by a dragon?

HELP!

Help is here!

SOMEONE'S IN THE KITCHEN

Cookies

Jimmy had great fun decorating these gingerbread men. Can you tell which two are EXACTLY alike? Be sure to look on both pages.

Serve It Up!

Can you find all twenty-six cooking terms in the grid?

```
T S Q H E A T Q T G
P L T A S T E U S H
P I K C A R C H O P
R C R O L L H O P R
E E T L E M I S O J
H M S B O I L P U K
E Q E H A X L R R S
A A R A U K S I F T
T Q V U S N E N W U
S A E T I U F K A F
Q S I M M E R L S F
K R W H I P Y E H I
```

BAKE
BEAT
BOIL
CHILL
CHOP
COOK
CRACK
CUT
FRY
HEAT
MEASURE
MELT
MIX
POUR
PREHEAT
ROLL
SERVE
SIFT
SIMMER
SLICE
SPRINKLE
STIR
STUFF
TASTE
WASH
WHIP

Totally Tablespoons

Margarita is baking a cake. The recipe calls for:

* 2 cups of flour

* 1 1/2 cups of sugar

* 1/4 cup of cocoa

Unfortunately, Margarita only has a tablespoon with which to measure. Do you know how many tablespoons (Tbsp.) she will need for each ingredient?

Hint: 1 cup = 16 Tbsp.

Flour = _____Tbsp.

Sugar = _____Tbsp.

Cocoa = _____Tbsp.

Mystery Meals

Someone forgot to tell us what they are cooking! Can you tell what each recipe will make from reading the list of ingredients? Write the name of the finished food at the top of each card.

Here's What's Cookin': _____

1/2 cup butter
1 cup brown sugar
2 eggs
1 1/2 tsp. vanilla
2 1/2 cups flour
1 tsp. baking soda
1/2 tsp. salt
6 oz. semi-sweet chocolate pieces

Here's What's Cookin': _____

1 head lettuce
cherry tomatoes
1 cucumber
2 carrots
1 green pepper
4 radishes
onion
Italian Dressing

Here's What's Cookin': _____

8 cups water
1 3/4 cups uncooked macaroni
8 oz. cheddar cheese
1/4 cup flour
2 cups milk
dash of pepper

Fast 'n' Funny
What stays hot even if you put it in the refrigerator?

Pepper!

Here's What's Cookin': _____

8 slices bread
2 eggs
butter
1/2 cup milk
1 Tbsp. sugar
1/4 tsp. cinnamon
maple syrup

Fast 'n' Funny
What tastes better before it is cooked?

Burnt toast!

79

ZOOEY ZOO

Seeing Double

The animals with double letters in their names have gotten all mixed up. Can you straighten them out? Move the double letters from one animal to another until all the animals make sense again!

1. OORDVARK = _ _ RDVARK

2. KANGAREE = KANGAR _ _

3. MONGAASE = MONG _ _ SE

4. RASSIT = RA _ _ IT

5. OPOPPUM = OPO_ _ UM

6. GIRABBE = GIRA _ _ E

7. GIRRON = GI _ _ ON

8. HIFFO = HI _ _ O

9. PABBOT = PA _ _ OT

Fast 'n' Funny
What do you call two bananas?

A pair of slippers!

Fast 'n' Funny
What two flowers can be found at the zoo?

Dandelion and Tiger Lily!

Color-a-Message

Color in every letter that is <u>not</u> a Z to find a special message from the zookeeper.

```
Z  Z  P  Z  L
E  Z  Z  Z  A
Z  S  Z  Z  E
D  Z  Z  O  Z
N  Z  Z  Z  Z
Z  O  T  Z  F
Z  Z  E  Z  Z
E  Z  Z  D  Z
T  H  Z  Z  Z
Z  E  A  Z  N
Z  I  M  Z  Z
A  Z  Z  L  S
```

Zack's Favorite

Fill in all the triangles to show the path to Zack's favorite animal. When you're done, finish each of the signs with Zack's favorite letter. Can you guess what it is?

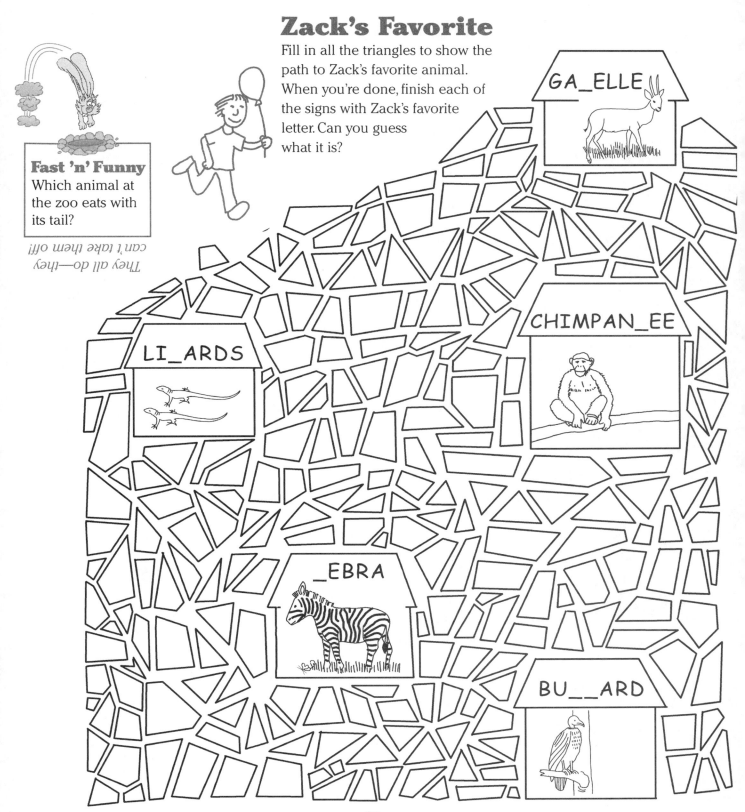

GA_ELLE

CHIMPAN_EE

LI_ARDS

_EBRA

BU__ARD

CREEPY CRAWLIES

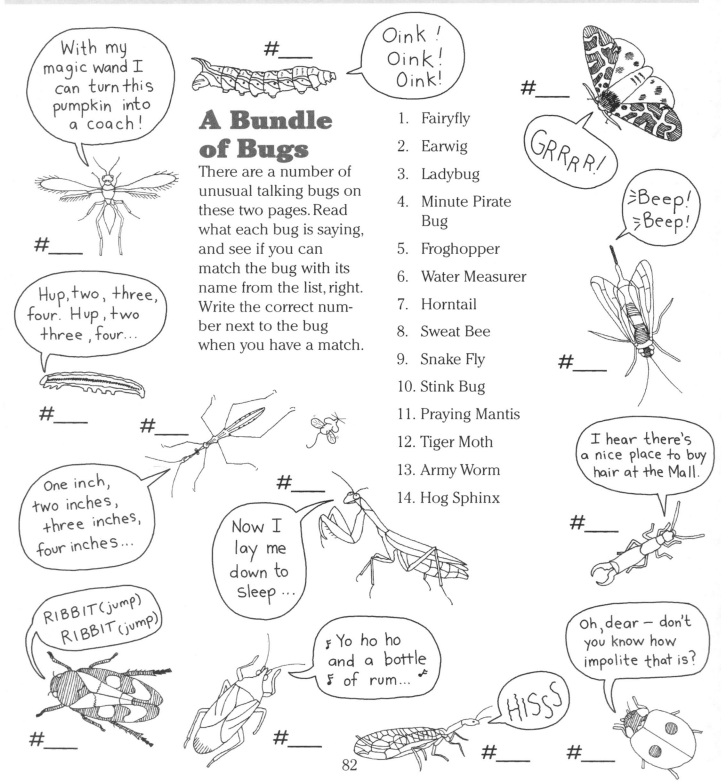

A Bundle of Bugs

There are a number of unusual talking bugs on these two pages. Read what each bug is saying, and see if you can match the bug with its name from the list, right. Write the correct number next to the bug when you have a match.

1. Fairyfly
2. Earwig
3. Ladybug
4. Minute Pirate Bug
5. Froghopper
6. Water Measurer
7. Horntail
8. Sweat Bee
9. Snake Fly
10. Stink Bug
11. Praying Mantis
12. Tiger Moth
13. Army Worm
14. Hog Sphinx

With my magic wand I can turn this pumpkin into a coach!

#___

Hup, two, three, four. Hup, two three, four...

#___

One inch, two inches, three inches, four inches...

#___

RIBBIT (jump) RIBBIT (jump)

#___

#___

Now I lay me down to sleep...

#___

Yo ho ho and a bottle of rum...

#___

#___

Oink! Oink! Oink!

#___

GRRRR!

#___

Beep! Beep!

#___

I hear there's a nice place to buy hair at the Mall.

#___

HISSS

#___

Oh, dear — don't you know how impolite that is?

#___

82

Mixed-Up Metamorphosis

Everybody knows that caterpillars change into butterflies. But did you know that a butterfly can become a firefly? You can do it in four steps if you make the right compound words.

BUTTERFLY to

FLY_____ to

_____ to

_____ to

FIREFLY

Itsy Bitsy

A pictograph is a very simple drawing — kind of like visual shorthand. Can you guess what this little pictograph shows?

Charlotte's Riddle

Start at the T marked with the spiders. Read the letters in a spiral toward the center to find the answer to this riddle: What day is it when two spiders get married?

Boy, am I HOT!

#__

Fast 'n' Funny

What does a bee say when he comes back to the hive?

Hi, honey, I'm home!

Hiding in a Honeycomb

There are six bugs hiding in this honeycomb. Can you find them? Start at any letter and move one space at a time in any direction. Once you've found all the bugs, see what other words you can make.

I don't know why I'm way over here. I don't smell <u>that</u> bad!

#__

Letters in honeycomb: B E T L E T E A N T E D L U G F L D B Y

83

Tools of the Trade

Can you find eight things that don't belong in this garden?

Pick a Bouquet

Iris wants to pick flowers for her friends. Use two straight lines to divide this flower bed into four equal bunches. Each bouquet should have the same amount of tulips, roses, and daisies.

Bee to Flower

How can you get the bee to land on the flower?

84

Mixed-Up Garden

Unscramble each of the words in this garden. Write your answers in the rows provided. When you are finished, read the letters under the garden hoops from top to bottom. You will see that all these plants have something in common.

They are all

_____ .

DINVEE

CREUUBCM

NTELPGGA

EANB

OAPTOT

ARROCT

LOCIBCOR

LUTETCE

PPERPE

PNHCASI

Herbal Seed Packets

Using straight lines only, finish the letters on these seed packets to form the names of some familiar herbs.

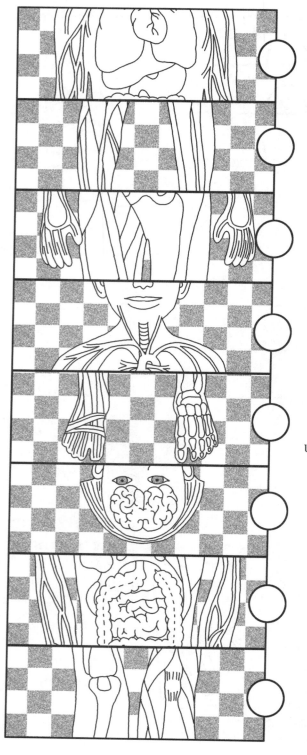

The Inner You

Whoa—the body on the left is all mixed-up! See if you can number the body parts in the correct order to match the picture on the right. The head is number one. Be careful— some of the pieces are upside down!

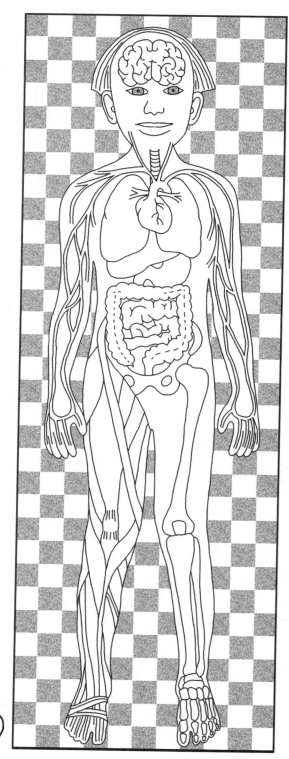

It All Makes Sense

Use your brain to figure out these small picture clues.
The shaded row tells you what they are called as a
group. We left you some E's for your Excellent Effort!

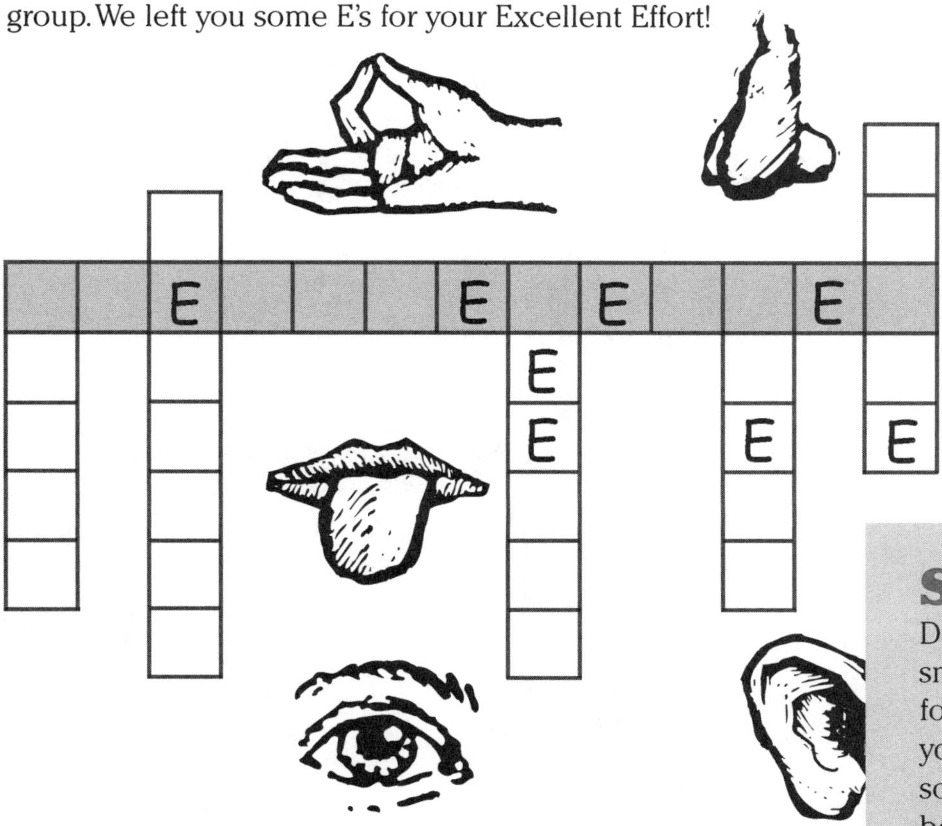

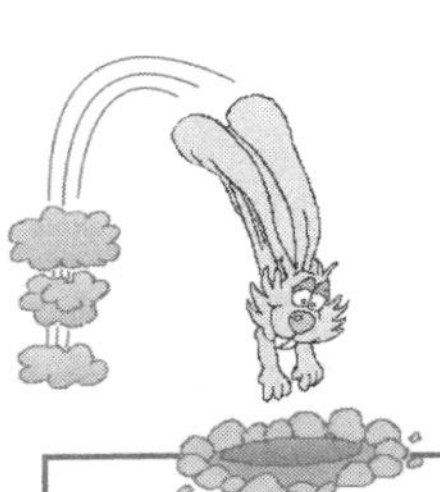

E E E E E

E

E

E E

Body Scramble

Unscramble the names of each part of the body, then put them in order from head to toes.

OTES _____ #__   DAEH _____ #__

SWAIT _____ #__   STECH _____ #__

GLES _____ #__   SHIP _____ #__

CKNE _____ #__   EFET _____ #__

DOSHULRES _____ #__

WILD WEATHER

ACROSS

4. This goes under a leak in the roof

6. Your puppy makes these on the rug, and a rainstorm makes them on the sidewalk

9. 28 Across will keep your feet _____ while sloshing through puddles

11. To wear away by the action of wind, rain, ice, etc.

12. Too much rainwater in a river will cause a _____

14. If you don't use a 25 Down in a rainstorm, you'll get _____

15. You wear these to protect your eyes on a sunny day

17. This keeps your head warm on a cold winter's day

18. A rain _____ helps keep you dry in a storm

19. You'll need one of these if it rains for 40 days and 40 nights

20. Drops of water falling from the clouds

22. This thick water vapor stays close to the ground and is hard to see through

26. Rain and dirt make _____

27. During a drought is a perfect time for a forest _____ to start

28. You need these to slosh through puddles

30. This ocean forms many powerful tropical storms

31. A very strong wind

33. You'll need one of these after a big snowstorm

34. Cloth comes in "bolts," and so does this form of electricity

36. A disturbance in the atmosphere that causes wind, rain, snow, etc.

38. Sailors will blow a special _____ when it is foggy so that other boats won't run into them

40. A REALLY big snowstorm

42. Some people say this is the sound of men bowling in the clouds

43. Frozen rain

44. After a long rain, the ground gets full of water and _____

DOWN

1. One of these won't keep a river from flooding, but many might

2. Moisture that collects on the grass in the early morning

3. Freezing rain

4. An inlet of the sea, usually protected from storms. Many people bring their boats into a _____ during a hurricane

5. Another word for tornado

88

7. This frozen water comes in flakes, not cubes

8. Waves caused by a storm at sea can erode _____ and cause houses to fall into the ocean

10. Yet another name for a tornado

13. A very, very light rain

15. You wear this in the winter to keep your neck warm

16. Sometimes your roof will do this in a rainstorm

17. Small balls of ice that fall from the clouds

18. When the sky is overcast, we say it is a _____ day

21. This powerful storm has its eye on you!

23. Wear these on your hands if you are out making snowballs

24. A tiny whirlwind full of sand is called a "_____ devil"

25. These can blow inside-out in a strong wind

27. A beautiful day with no clouds is called _____ weather

29. All the weather in this puzzle takes place in the atmosphere on the planet _____

31. A strong outburst of wind

32. When rain comes down very heavy and fast

35. A violent whirlwind with a funnel-shaped cloud

36. You usually put these on your bed, but a heavy rain can also fall in _____

37. Sometimes during a flood you can see people _____ boats down the middle of their street

38. The three H's of summer are ____, hot, and humid

39. On a fair day, the sky is a lovely shade of _____

41. Sometimes after a blizzard, people have to ____ their way out of their houses

Tons O' Twisters / Did you know that the most tornadoes EVER happened right here in the US? There was a total of 148 tornadoes that swept through the southern and midwestern part of the country on April 3rd and 4th in 1974. YIKES!

Forever Forecasting

Here's the twelve-day forecast — but the weather person forgot to write what kind of weather the symbols stand for! Can you match the weather descriptions with their weather symbols? Write the descriptions on the lines provided. Make sure the first letter of each description goes in the circle.

Terrific Day

Mostly Sunny

Overcast

Rainy

Light Wind

Gusts of Wind

Emergency Weather Watch

Ice & Sleet

Sunny

Now, read all the letters in the circles. They will spell the professional title of a person who studies the atmosphere, weather, and weather forecasting.

89

New Neighbors

Each member of the Thomas family has a sign. Follow the directions below to find out the message they have for their new neighbors.

1. Fill in all the blocks on the left side of each person's sign.

2. Fill in all the top blocks on Gramma, Jesse, Dad, and Sally's signs.

3. Fill in all the blocks on the right side of Rachel, Mom, and Dad's signs.

4. Fill in the center block on Mom, Gramma, Rachel, and Sally's signs.

5. Fill in the bottom block in columns 2 & 4 of Mom's sign. Also fill in the block just below the center in Mom's sign.

6. Fill in the second block from the top in columns 2 & 4 on Rachel's sign.

7. Fill in all the bottom blocks on Gramma, Chrissy, Jesse, and Sally's signs.

8. Fill in the remaining square on the bottom row of Dad's sign.

90

All Over Town

Here is a list of errands your mother asked you to do today. Mom reminds you to do the grocery shopping last so the milk won't spoil. If you start at your house, in what order should you do the errands to get them finished as quickly as possible? When you have figured out the fastest route, number the errands on the list correctly from first to last.

Hint: Count the spaces from one place to the next to see which way is the shortest. The "driveway" for each parking lot counts as one square.

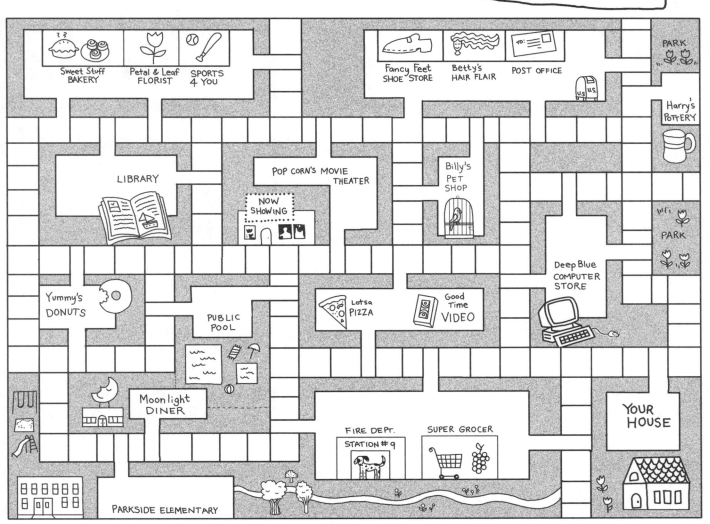

ONLY OPPOSITES

Opposites Crossword

Figure out the answers to the questions below and fill them into the numbered crossword grid. All the answers will be the opposite of the clues. Bad Curse! (Oops, that should be "Good Luck!")

ACROSS

1. Opposite of friend

3. Opposite of bottom

6. Opposite of frown

7. Opposite of dry

9. Opposite of E.A.T.
    (Estimated Arrival Time)
    HINT: If the question is an acronym or abbreviation, the answer will be an acronym or abbreviation, too.

10. Opposite of happy

12. Opposite of disarm
    (take away weapons)

14. Opposite of unusual

15. Opposite of getting up is going to _ _ _

16. Opposite of followed
    HINT: Remember, if the clue is in the past tense, the answer must be in the past tense, too.

DOWN

1. Opposite of many

2. Suffix that means the opposite of the least. HINT: If something is the opposite of the least tall, it is the tall _ _ _

3. Opposite of untie

4. Opposite of younger

5. Opposite of an animal that is wild

8. Opposite of write down

10. A prefix that is the opposite of over
    HINT: A "_ _ _ marine" goes under the water.

11. Opposite of a thing that works correctly

12. Opposite of none

13. Opposite of not angry

92

Say Again?

Can you translate this silly conversation? Above each underlined word or group of words, write a word that means the opposite.

"Hey <u>here</u>, Jason!"

"<u>Goodbye</u>, Aaron!"

"How are <u>me</u>?"

"<u>You</u> <u>haven't</u> a <u>good</u> <u>hot</u>."

"How <u>wonderful</u>! I hope you <u>give</u> <u>worse</u> <u>a long time from now</u>."

"<u>You</u>, too. I <u>did</u> <u>wake</u> <u>none</u> <u>day</u> <u>short</u>."

"Oh, that's too <u>good</u>. Well, <u>you</u> <u>haven't</u> to <u>come</u>. <u>Hello</u>!"

"<u>Hello</u>. See <u>me</u> <u>sooner</u>."

Shifting Shadows

Which of the figures is the EXACT opposite of each figure in the box below? Draw a line between each pair of pattern partners.

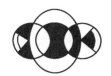

1.

2.

3.

4.

What Was That?

It is awfully noisy around here! Can you figure out all these noises? Listen carefully…we left you a H-O-W-L and a B-U-M-P in the night.

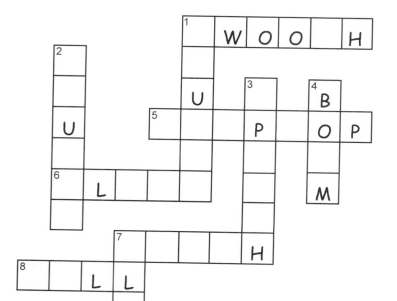

ACROSS

1. Low-flying bat
5. Frog falling in a pond
6. Two glasses hitting lightly
7. A big metal tray falling on the floor
8. Call for help
9. Door slamming shut

DOWN

1. Rusty door
2. Shoes stepping on glass
3. Bag of money being thrown in a lake
4. Explosion
7. Something being hit

I Spy

Can you find the CLUES hidden inside the grid? There is only one time that all five letters appear in a row. Look forward, backward, up and down, and diagonally. It could be anywhere!

```
S C E E S U L S C S
C L U S U L C L U C
L U L U C E S C E S
S S C L L S E U C L
U C S C U C L U S U
E E L E L C S C U E
C S U E U C L E L S
S L C S E L E U C L
C S U L C U C L E S
E L C E S E L C L U
```

Fast 'n' Funny
Here's another strange noise for you—what goes "HA HA HA BUMP"?

Someone laughing their head off!

94

What's Wrong?

Circle the twenty things that seem odd or out of place in this room.

Calling Code

Susan is calling her friends to invite them to a party. Using the phone keypad as a decoder, figure out the names of the people invited. Each phone button has several letters on it, so be sure to look for the number after the slash. It tells you if the letter is in the second or third space. For example, 2/2 = B. A number with no slash after it means the letter is in the first space.

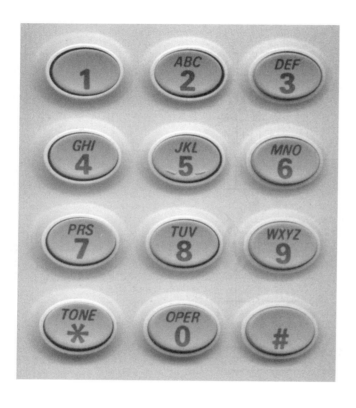

1. 4/3-6-2   6/2-8/2-8-8

   _____

2. 3/3-7/2-2-6/2-5/2

   _____

   6/2   7/3-8-3/2-4/3-6/2

   _____

3. 8-3/2-3   3/2   2/2-3/2-2-7/2

   _____

4. 8-2-3/3-3/3-9/3   7-8/2-5/3-5/3

   _____

5. 3-7/2-3/2-9   2   2/2-6/3-2-8

   _____

6. 7/3-8/2-6-6-3/2-7/2   8-4/3-6-3/2

   _____

7. 7/3-2-6/2-8-2   2/3-5/3-2-8/2-7/3

   _____

Cut the Cake

How would you cut a round cake into nine pieces with only four cuts of a knife?

Good Games

Read the clues carefully and see how many party games you can fit into the crossword grid. We wished you a H-A-P-P-Y B-I-R-T-H-D-A-Y as a hint!

ACROSS

2. Players hop in a bag to the finish line

3. Teams of players balance a small food item on a metal object

4. Pairs of players try to throw a delicate food item as far as possible without breaking it

7. Players retrieve handkerchief from "enemy" territory

10. Players try to pass under an ever-lower stick

11. Players pass the spud as quickly as they can

13. Players are blindfolded and try to attach a missing piece to an animal picture

15. Players must listen carefully and follow the leader's directions

16. Players swing a stick to try and get treats

17. Players must run while tied to their partner

18. One player walks on hands while their partner holds ankles

DOWN

1. Players must stay still when tapped by the leader

2. Players search for all the items on a list

5. Players ask permission to take long strides toward the leader

6. Players try to capture wet fruit with their teeth

8. Players stop and start as certain color words are called

9. Players race for empty places to sit

12. Players are "out" when a light is shined on them

14. Players pass a whispered phrase, trying to keep it correct

I CAN'T BELIEVE MY EYES!

Optical illusions are a kind of puzzle designed to fool your eyes. See if you can tell the difference between illusion and reality in the following popular optical illusions.

1. Do you see a <u>13</u> or a <u>B</u> in the center of the figures above?

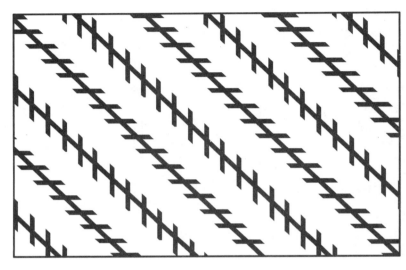

2. Are the long black lines parallel (even) with each other, or are they crooked?

3. Do you see two faces — or a vase?

4. Which of these girls is the tallest?

5. How many planks do you see?

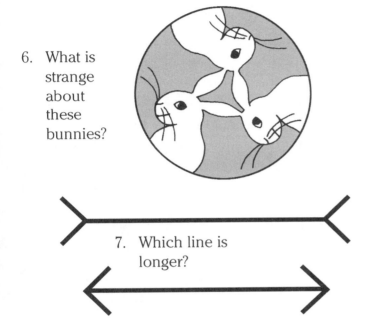

6. What is strange about these bunnies?

7. Which line is longer?

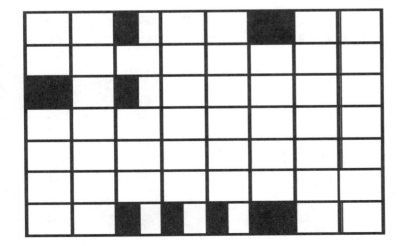

8. Can you read the secret message?

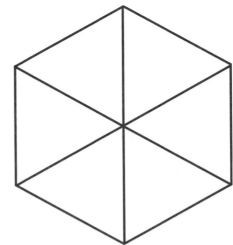

9. Is this a hexagon — or can you see something else?

10. What do you see where the white lines cross?

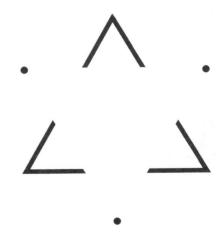

11. Can you see the white triangle?

PLUNDERING PIRATES

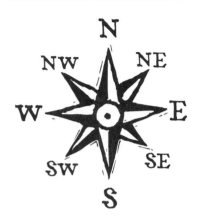

X Marks the Spot

Treasure could be buried at any of the X spots on this map. Using the compass and following the directions below, you should be able to find the right one.

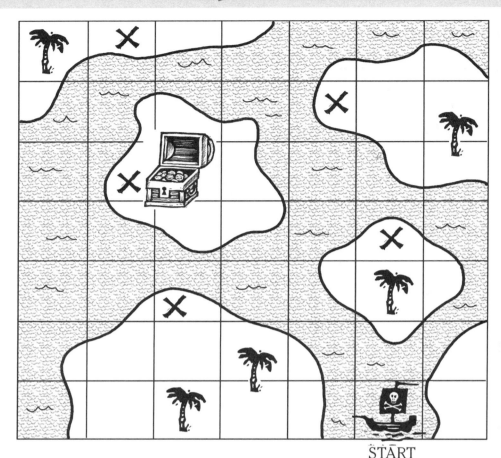

START

N one block
NW one block
N two blocks
NW two blocks
SW two blocks
E one block

Dividing the Booty

Captain Jack and his crew are dividing up their treasure. Using the information given below, can you figure out how many gold coins each pirate will get?

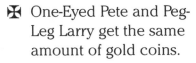

✠ One-Eyed Pete and Peg-Leg Larry get the same amount of gold coins.

✠ Captain Jack gets half of the total treasure.

✠ Each pirate's share can be divided by the number five.

✠ The total treasure is 50 gold coins.

Captain Jack gets _____ coins

One-Eyed Pete gets _____ coins

Barnacle Bill gets _____ coins

Peg-Leg Larry gets _____ coins

Walk the Plank

Can you fill in the blanks for these words that also end in the letters A-N-K?

1. A pirate would probably not deposit his money in a
— — — — —.

2. Stealing a pirate's wooden leg and replacing it with an umbrella might be considered a silly
— — — — — —.

3. Pirates probably __ __ __ __ __ because they couldn't bathe very often.

4. On board a pirate ship they might use a __ __ __ __ __ __ to turn a wheel.

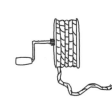

5. If pirates __ __ __ __ __ __ sea water, they would get really sick.

6. Many pirate ships __ __ __ __ during a bad storm or after a battle.

Places of Worship

Throughout the week, people of all religions gather to worship. Can you fit the names of seven places of worship into the grid? We left you some beautiful M-U-S-I-C as a hint.

Household Chores

Find an action word in the list to fit with each of these items. Write it on the line in front of the item and you will have a long list of common household chores. How many of them do you do at home?

1. _____ floor

2. _____ dishes

3. _____ table

4. _____ rugs

5. _____ furniture

6. _____ newspapers

7. _____ trash cans

8. _____ laundry

9. _____ sink

10. _____ plants

11. _____ meals

12. _____ pets

Word List

wash	recycle	sweep
feed	empty	fold
vacuum	water	cook
scrub	dust	set

After-School Activities

James is very busy after school. Using the clues below, figure out on which day of the week he has each activity planned. Fill in the calendar at the bottom of this page for James.

✎ He plans to go to the library three days before his piano lesson.

✎ He has a swimming lesson two days after his baseball game.

✎ He is going to the movies with Tim at the end of the week.

✎ His piano lesson is scheduled on Thursday.

✎ His scout meeting is the day before his swimming lesson.

✎ He will go to the library and the baseball game on the same day.

Weekly Maze

Can you start at the word "Monday" on the calendar below and work your way through the WEEK until you reach Friday?

Monday	Tuesday	Wednesday	Thursday	Friday

MONSTER MASH

An Ugly Crowd

Can you use two straight lines to divide this group of monsters into four equal groups? Each group should have eight monster <u>heads</u>. Your line can go over the tips of tails or feet, but <u>not</u> through any bodies or necks!

Scared?

Did you know there's a word that means "fear of monsters"? Use the decoder to read the monster's eyes and see what this scary word is.

A   B   E   H   I   O   P   R   T

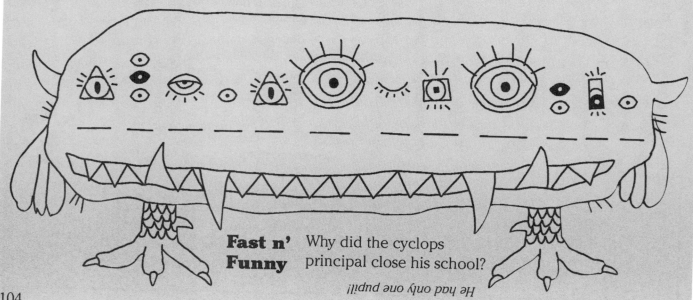

Fast n' Funny   Why did the cyclops principal close his school?

He had only one pupil!

Late at Night

How much do you know about those creepy creatures in late night movies and TV shows?

ACROSS

2. What do you call a crazy vampire?

4. The sound of a lightning bolt

6. "The _____" is a monster with no particular shape, but a big appetite

9. This is the name of a doctor who brought a famous monster to life

11. A famous Egyptian monster

12. "The Creature from the Black _____"

13. You might confuse this big green monster with a dinosaur

16. Dr. Jekyll's evil monster twin

18. "7 Down" climbed to the ____ of the Empire State Building

20. Vampires must be home by this time of day

21. This gentle blue monster lives on Sesame Street and loves crunchy, sweet treats

DOWN

1. A monster who should be dead but is still walking around

3. If this monster was smaller, you would swat it!

5. "The _____ of the Opera" is now a popular musical monster

6. A mad scientist's laboratory is always being hit by _____ of lightning

7. A super-giant-gorilla-monster

8. The most famous movie vampire

10. This monster needs to shave when the moon is full

14. Many TV stations show monster movies _____ at night

15. This type of scientist is always making monsters

17. What you yell when you run into a monster

19. Wolfman leaves ____ prints when he walks

Way to Grow

This monster is growing eyes — and other parts, too! Figure out the pattern, then draw the correct number of eyes on the last head!

GOING ON A PICNIC

Having Fun

There are many ways to amuse yourself on a picnic. In each of the following, the words making up an activity have been squished together. Can you figure them all out?

1. FLKIYTE   _ _ _   _ _ _ _

2. EAFOOTD   _ _ _   _ _ _ _

3. REBADOOK   _ _ _ _   _ _ _ _

4. TANAKEP   _ _ _ _   _ _ _

5. WADOLKG   _ _ _ _   _ _ _

6. CLITREMEB   _ _ _ _ _   _ _ _ _

7. THBROWALL   _ _ _ _ _   _ _ _ _

8. PLACAYRDS   _ _ _ _   _ _ _ _ _

Ready to Go

Look carefully at the picnic scene, below. Figure out what object is by each number and write that word in the spaces provided. Then, take the circled letters and unscramble them. They will spell the answer to this riddle:

You bring me to the picnic, and I bring the picnic with me. What am I?

1. ◯ _ _ _ ◯ _ _

2. _ ◯ _ _ ◯ _ _ _

3. ◯ _ ◯ _ ◯

4. _ _ ◯ _ ◯ _ _

5. _ ◯ _ _ _ ◯ _ _

6. _ _ _ _ ◯

Answer: _ _ _ _ _ _ _

_ _ _ _ _ _

106

Ants

Help the ants find their way across the blanket to the picnic. Stop at all the sweet treats, but go past the silverware.

Start

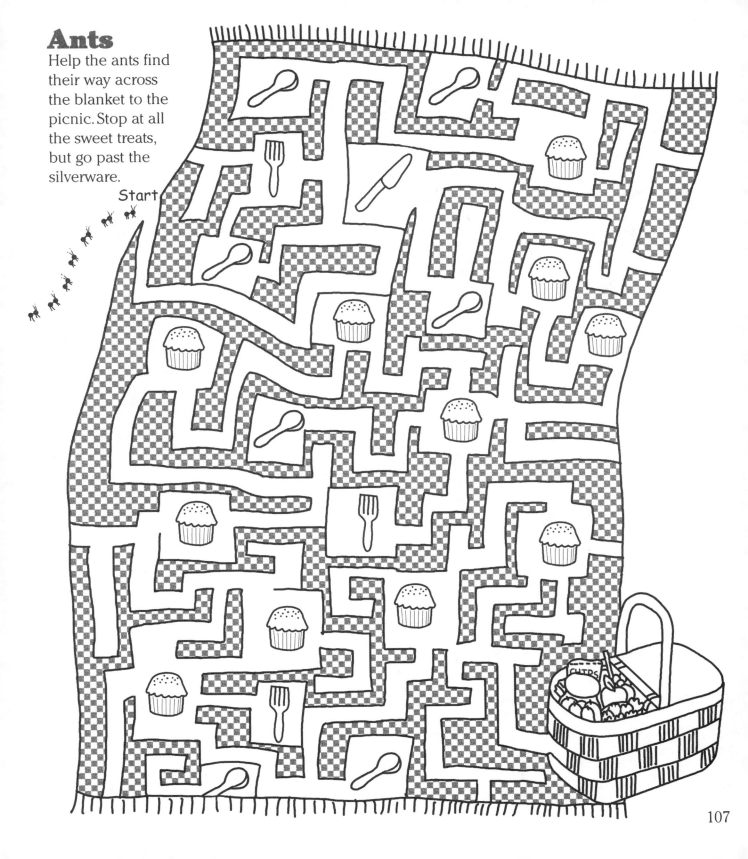

107

HERE COMES THE CIRCUS

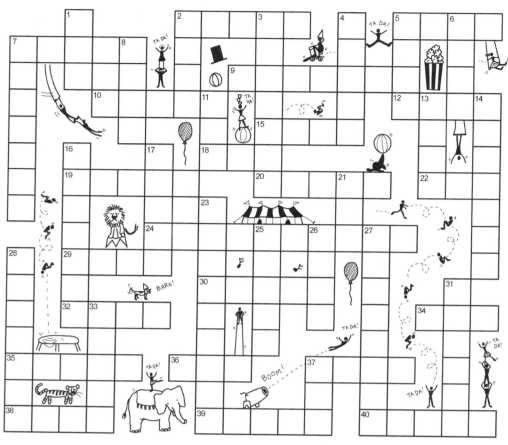

37. After an exciting act, the crowd will _____ and whistle

38. A trained acrobat makes a difficult trick look _____

39. Many of the circus acts are _____-duper!

40. This performer always wears stripes

DOWN

1. A tent _____ is a little piece of wood that holds the tent ropes in the ground

2. Some clowns will sneak up behind you and honk a loud _____

3. You have to feed a lot of these to number 26 Down

4. This performer's specialty is to make you laugh

5. The circus _____ plays all different kinds of music

6. The lion is also known as the "_____" of beasts.

7. This is a favorite circus snack — do you like yours with butter?

8. It's funny to see a clown _____ on banana peels!

11. Some circuses have a "_____ lion" that will balance a big ball on his nose

13. What one acrobat says when he drops another acrobat

ACROSS

2. Lions and tigers often jump through _____

5. It's funny to see a BIG clown riding a little, teeny, weeny _____

7. Have you ever seen a clown slip on banana _____?

9. It's fun to get a helium _____ at the circus

10. These performers are one of the "mane" events at the circus

12. Circus _____ will bark when they are told to

15. Some acrobats perform high ___ ___ the trapeze (two words)

18. Each different performance of the circus is called an _____

19. Clowns love to have a big, noisy _____ to perform for

20. Acrobats _____ back and forth on the trapeze several times before they fly through the air

22. Some clowns are happy, and some are _____

24. He is the man in a top hat and red coat who directs the circus

29. It is hard for an acrobat to balance on top of a rolling _____

30. The lions and tigers must be _____, or they might eat the clowns!

32. The circus takes place inside a big _____

34. The circus tent is also called "The Big ___"

35. Wouldn't it be fun if they needed an _____ clown, and the ringmaster asked you?

36. The first line of an old circus song goes "They _____ through the air with the greatest of ease..."

108

14. They fill the circus rings with _____ to keep it nice and soft

16. This performer can bounce and flip and jump

17. Some fancy jugglers will _____ dinner plates on top of long sticks

21. There is a big _____ under the high wire in case an acrobat falls

23. Some acrobats ride these one wheelers up on the high wire

25. Some circus tricks are so amazing, they look like _____

26. You might drink a big, cold _____ if it's a hot day at the circus

27. They are the biggest performers of them all!

28. With 35 Across, the second part of a circus song goes "...those daring young men on the flying _____"

31. Some acrobats will _____ on a trampoline

33. You better get to the circus _____ to get a good seat

37. It is funny to see fifteen or twenty clowns pile out of a tiny _____

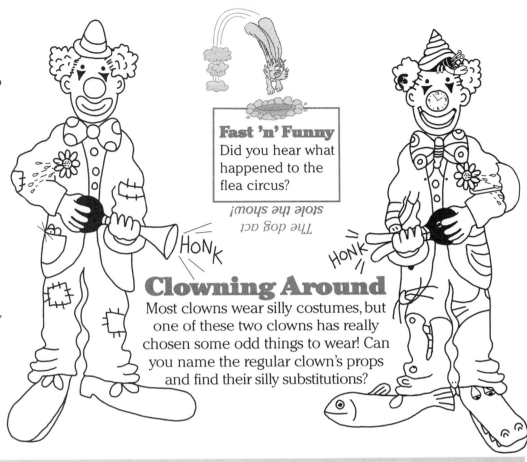

Clowning Around

Most clowns wear silly costumes, but one of these two clowns has really chosen some odd things to wear! Can you name the regular clown's props and find their silly substitutions?

HONK   HONK

Tricky Tongue Twisters

A clever clown stole the vital vowels from these tricky tongue twisters. Can you supply them — and say each tongue twister three times fast?

1. _L_G_NT

   _L_PH_NTS

2. J_LLY

   J_GGL_RS

   J_GGL_

   J_LLY J_RS

3. TW_

   T_WNY

   T_G_RS

   TR_V_L

   TW_TCH_NG

   T_GHTR_P_S

   T_G_TH_R

4. _ _R_ _L

   _CR_B_TS

   _CC_MPL_SH

   _BS_L_T_LY

   _M_Z_NG

   _CTS

   _B_V_

   _N

   _W_STR_CK

   _ _D_ _NC_

109

VROOM, VROOM!

Word Wheel

Start at the letter B marked with a white dot. Move clockwise around the circle picking up every third letter. Write them on the lines below. When you have finished, you will find the answer to this riddle:

Why are sleepy people like automobile wheels?

__ __ __ __ __ __ __

__ __ __ __ __

__ __ __

__ __ __ __ __!

Wheelin' Around

Using the small pictures as clues, can you fill this groupie with some familiar vehicles that have wheels? We have left you some V-R-O-O-Ms as a hint.

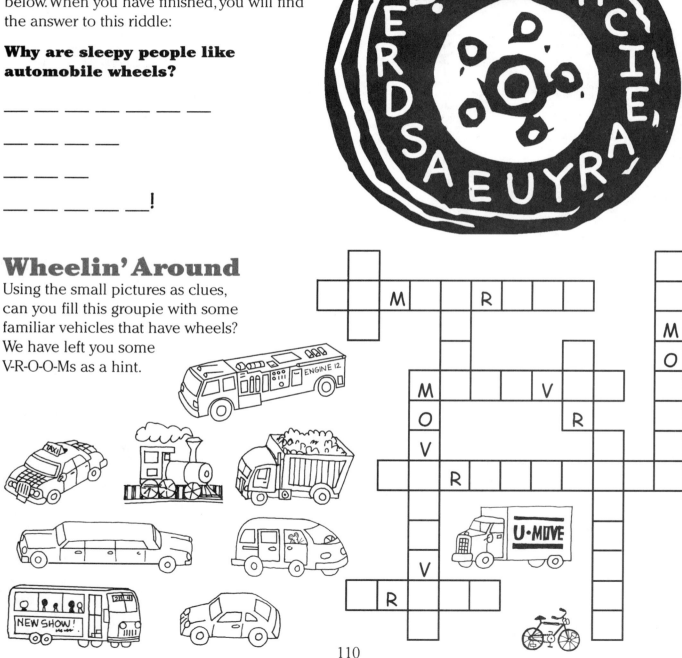

110

Vanity Plates

Some license plates tell a lot about their owners. Can you match the following people with their license plate? Write the correct owner under each plate.

Mom	Santa Claus
Newlyweds	Tennis Player
Clown	Star Trek Fan
Computer Wiz	Math Teacher
Pretty Girl	Artist

ICR8

HOHOHO

2PLS2Z4

HRDDRV

TNSNY1

IMFUNE

5KDZ

IDOLUVU

QTPIE

BMMEUP

Skid Marks

These tire tracks tell a lot about what the owner of each vehicle does. Draw a line to match each vehicle with its tracks.

climbs mountains

bird watcher

curls hair

delivers flowers

surfs

fishes

111

IT'S TREE-MENDOUS!

Tallest Tree

You will be reading the growth rings on this tree stump in a clockwise direction. Start at the letter in the center ring marked with a black dot. Read around the ring until you reach the black dot again. Then, jump out to the next ring and continue reading in a clockwise direction. When you are finished you will know the answer to the question:

What is the tallest tree?

Properly Pronounced

Each type of tree here is listed by its dictionary pronunciation. Watch your spelling as you write each one correctly in the space provided.

1. mā′pəl _____

2. bēch _____

3. ōk _____

4. sprüs _____

5. bûrch _____

6. päm _____

7. wil′ō _____

8. fûr _____

9. jü′nə pər _____

10. mə hog′ə nē _____

11. pop′lər _____

12. sē′dər _____

13. bôl′səm _____

14. hik′ə rē _____

112

Good Things Grow on Trees

Circle those things that grow on trees.

Cross out the things that
DO NOT grow on trees.

Shade in those items that
are made from trees!

Fast 'n' Funny
What is a tree's
favorite game?

Follow the cedar!

Fast 'n' Funny
What does a tree
yell at sporting
events?

I'm rooting for you!

SNOW DAY

Bundle Up!

ACROSS

Unscramble these winter clothing words and write them in the crossword grid.

2. TOBOS
3. SVELOG
4. STAPOWNNS
5. RAKAP
6. WERTEAS
7. ATH
8. CRAFS

DOWN

1. When you have filled in all the other words, see if you can guess this last important item of warm winter clothing!

Snow What?

Staring at 1, connect the dots to see what Beth made in her yard.

Hot Chocolate

Keith, Jon, and Adam have just come in from sledding. Using the following clues, can you figure out how many marshmallows each boy likes in his cocoa?

❋ Jon has three less marshmallows than Adam.

❋ There are nine marshmallows.

❋ Keith has twice as many marshmallows as Adam.

Jon __ Keith __ Adam __

Snowy Words

Do you know all of these words that begin with "snow"?

1. A packed sphere of snow ....SNOW _ _ _ _

2. One of these small ice crystals..............SNOW _ _ _ _ _

3. A person made out of snow ....SNOW _ _ _

4. A vehicle for traveling on snow ....SNOW _ _ _ _ _ _

5. Flat webbed frames attached
   to boots for walking on snow ....SNOW _ _ _ _ _

6. A heavy, curved metal blade
   used to push snow off the road ....SNOW _ _ _ _

7. Strong winds and heavy snow ....SNOW _ _ _ _ _

Fast 'n' Funny
Why does it snow
in the winter?

*Because snow would
melt in the summer!*

Similar Snowflakes

No two snowflakes are supposed to be exactly alike. But two of these are. Can you spot them?

PLAYING AT THE MOVIES

Popcorn Maze

Help Mervin get through this handful of popcorn.

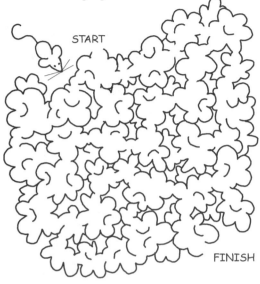

START

FINISH

Merry Poppin'

Popcorn isn't the only word with "pop" in it. How many of these words do you know that start with P-O-P?

1. Cartoon character who eats spinach to get strong .... **POP** _ _ _

2. Tall tree with wide leaves .... **POP** _ _ _

3. Garden plant with round red flowers .... **POP** _ _

4. Liked by many people .... **POP** _ _ _ _

5. Tradename for a frozen ice treat on two flat sticks .... **POP** _ _ _ _ _

Mystery Menu

You can get a really good deal at the refreshment counter if you can find the secret message hidden in the menu.

Fast 'n' Funny
What is a reptile's favorite movie?

The Lizard of Oz

refreshmenTs:

Water candy
Orange SODA nachoS
cofFee popcORn
hoT dog HamburgEr
Peanuts RICE cakes
cOla french Fries lemONadE

Secret Message: _____

Now Showing

Fill in the triangles on the screen to see what movie is being shown at the matinee today.

117

One Bird or Two?

Use this combinaton of pictures and letters to spell out a famous English proverb.

To Each Her Own

These birds are flying home to their nests. Using visual clues (size, shape, pattern), can you write each bird's number next to her nest?

Sunflower Snack

There are nine birds that like to eat sunflower seeds hidden in this puzzle. The first letter is provided for each one. Find the first letter of each in the grid and move one space at a time in any direction. You may use the same letter more than once, but not two times in a row.

```
U N A F D O D P O
G T H I N W O E C
N B C C A D E R K
I E L K R I N R A
D T F U G J A Y E
T M O T E G L P B
I T U S M R O S T
```

1. C _ _ _ _ _ _
2. C _ _ _ _ _ _ _ _
3. B _ _ _   _ _ _
4. T _ _ _ _ _

   _ _ _ _ _ _ _
5. G _ _ _ _ _ _
6. S _ _ _ _ _ _
7. F _ _ _ _
8. N _ _ _ _ _ _ _
9. W _ _ _ _ _ _ _ _ _

Two-Way Ducks

This strange flock of ducks can't seem to make up their minds — are they going left, or right? Can you figure out a simple way to get them going in one direction or the other?

Fast 'n' Funny
What cookie does a bird like best?

Chocolate Chirp!

119

The Last Word

This crazy crossword is all squashed together. Not only that, but you can spell some of the answers around corners, and even bottom to top! When you have filled in every square, read the letters from left to right. You will find a funny final message!

The Tail End

These animals are too shy to say goodbye, so they are hiding. But somehow their tails got mixed up with their noses! Draw a line between each happy tail and its proper nose. Can you name the animals, too?

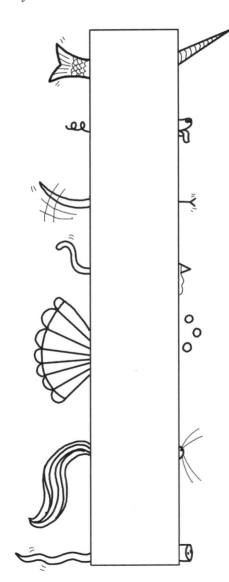

ACROSS

1. The begining of a famous USA song: "Oh say can you _____ ..."

4. The past tense of eat

6. The opposite of none

11. A casual way to say "no"

16. ROCK minus RK

20. The answer to a simple question can be either yes ___ ___ (two words)

DOWN

3. Shirts come in the following sizes: SM, MD and ___

5. A two letter abbreviation for railroad

8. To help

12. Santa usually says three of these in a row

14. Long distance truckers talk to each other on this kind of radio

UP

21. If you are going out with two friends, you would say "___ are leaving now."

AROUND THE CORNER

9. You have a big one on your foot

15. A popular sandwich is ham on _____

SINGLES

2. Q is always found with it

7. The ninth letter of the alphabet

10. The letter after H

13. "Hello" has two of these. Put one of them here

17. The letter before J

18. See 13 — put the other one here

19. The start of "finish"

Tasty Endings

A bit of dessert is a great end to a meal. Can you circle six favorites in the grid below? Then, read the leftover letters to find an end-of-day message!

```
D O C N S O I
T F O O U R C
B R O W N I E
G E K T D K C
T O I B A R R
U S E C E H E
T I H O S E A
P T E E T H M
```

Fast 'n' Funny

How does a bee say goodbye?

Gotta buzz!

How about a marathon racer?

Gotta run!

A gardener?

Seed you later!

A baseball player?

Catch you later!

A salesman?

Buy, buy!

A cheesemaker?

Gouda bye!

Bye, Mervin!

Mervin has finally reached the last page. Look what's waiting for him at the end of the maze! Help Mervin find his way to his new home as quickly as possible. He can follow the roads over and under. Do you think Mervin will be traveling again soon?

121

Answers

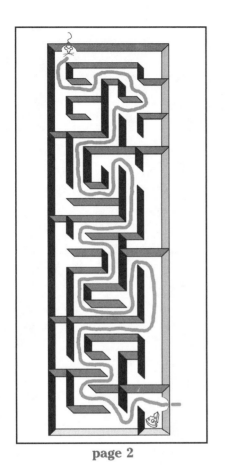

page 2

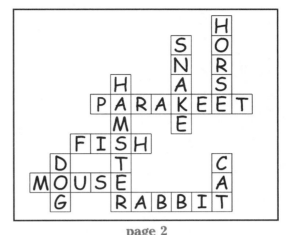

page 2

page 3

page 3

page 3

page 3

page 3

page 3

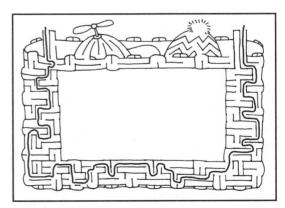

page 4

125

Answers

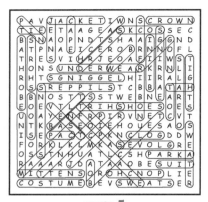

page 5

page 5

What's Different?
Answers:
1. Tag in back of coat different size
2. Different number of buttons down front of coat
3. Stripes on scarf in different order
4. Right mitten is in different direction
5. Zig-zag pattern at bottom of coat different
6. Bottom of pockets different shape
7. Different number of strings on left fringe of scarf
8. Mervin the mouse is in one of the pockets!

page 5

page 6

Hidden Presidents
Answers:
1. George Washington
2. Abraham Lincoln
3. Theodore Roosevelt
4. John F. Kennedy
5. Richard M. Nixon
6. Bill Clinton

page 6

Capitol Confusion
Correct answers: 1. 2. and 3.

page 6

Rebus for President
Answers:
1. Dwight D. Eisenhower
2. George Bush

page 7

page 8

Presidential Quotable Quote
Answers:
A. Person, place, or thing = NOUN
B. To fasten = LOCK
C. To hurry = RUSH
D. What a cow chews = CUD
E. Adult male human = MAN
F. Caterpillar case = COCOON
G. Building in which people live = HOUSE
H. Opposite of night = DAY
I. To move through the air with wings = FLY
J. A plaything = TOY
K. Pull Suddenly = YANK
L. A large number = MANY
M. Sound a dog makes = WOOF
N. To attempt = TRY
O. Abrupt = CURT
P. Unhappy = SAD
Q. In another direction = AWAY
R. Part of plant that grows underground = ROOT
S. Person trained to care for the sick = NURSE
T. Twelve inches = FOOT
U. Mixture of gases surrounding the Earth = AIR
V. Armed fighting between people = WAR

page 7

page 7

Answers

Fruit Salad

Answers:
1. blueberries
2. watermelon
3. cantaloupe
4. apples
5. bananas
6. grapes

page 8

Serve 'em Up

Answer: 2 to 4

page 9

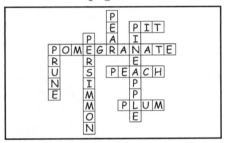

page 9

page 9

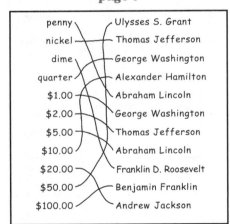

penny	Ulysses S. Grant
nickel	Thomas Jefferson
dime	George Washington
quarter	Alexander Hamilton
$1.00	Abraham Lincoln
$2.00	George Washington
$5.00	Thomas Jefferson
$10.00	Abraham Lincoln
$20.00	Franklin D. Roosevelt
$50.00	Benjamin Franklin
$100.00	Andrew Jackson

page 10

Loose Change

Answer: ceNTs

page 10

page 10

Answers

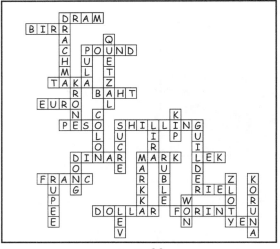

page 11

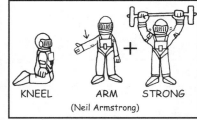

page 12

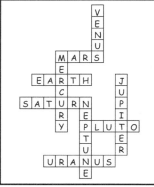

page 12

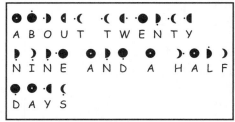

A B O U T   T W E N T Y

N I N E   A N D   A   H A L F

D A Y S

page 13

KNEEL   ARM   STRONG

(Neil Armstrong)

page 13

page 20

Color-a-Message
Answer:
In art the best is good enough.

page 20

Mixing Colors
Answers:

ROD = RED	GREET = GREEN
GLUE = BLUE	WINK = PINK
BLOCK = BLACK	CROWN = BROWN
GRANGE = ORANGE	WHINE = WHITE
MELLOW = YELLOW	MOLD = GOLD

page 20

Same Frames?
Answers:
Frames 1 and 5 are a pair.
Frames 2 and 6 are a pair.
Frames 3 and 4 are a pair.

page 21

Famous Artists
Answers:
1. Pablo Picasso
2. Claude Monet
3. Mary Cassatt
4. Georgia O'Keefe
5. Leonardo da Vinci
6. Vincent van Gogh

page 21

Answers

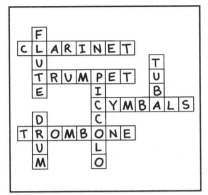

page 22

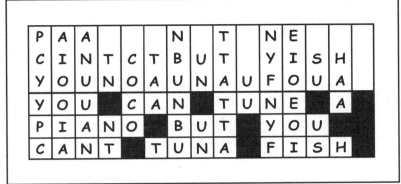

page 22

Classical Composers

Answers:
1. Johann Brahms
2. Peter Ilyich Tchaikovsky
3. Franz Joseph Haydn
4. Wolfgang Amadeus Mozart
5. Johann Sebastian Bach
6. Ludwig van Beethoven

page 23

Name That Tune

Answers:
1. Go In and Out the Window
2. It's a Small World

page 23

Read the Music

Answer:
He who sings drives away sorrow.

page 23

Whose Teeth Are These?

Answers:
1. shark (By the way, did you know that sharks can have as many as 24,000 teeth in their lifetime? When one falls out they just grow another one!)
2. child
3. beaver
4. grandma or grandpa!
5. dog
6. Marvin the mouse!
7. snake
8. vampire

page 24

Tiny Teeth

Answer: A buck-toothed clam!

page 24

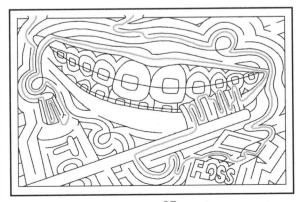

page 25

Mystery Words

Answers:
Brush your teeth after every meal.
Floss often to clean between teeth.
Limit sweets to avoid getting cavities.
Visit your dentist for regular checkups.

The circled letters spell the word SMILE

page 25

Answers

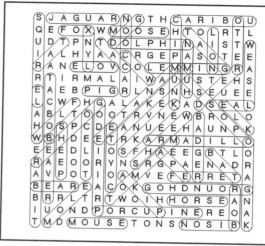

page 26

page 26

Practice Your Paw-menship

Answer:

The note reads "Dear Robin, Can you play baseball later? Would Chuck (woodchuck) lend you his bat (bat)? We'll go for (gopher) pizza, too. Tell your mom we ought to (otter) be home by six. Later, Martin (marten)."

Extra Info: Are you familiar with the animal called a "marten"? It is a sleek and furry mammal that looks like a very large weasle.

page 27

What Are These?

Answers:

1. Armadillo
2. Bat
3. Beaver
4. Deer
5. Dolphin
6. Mole
7. Opossum
8. Porcupine
9. Rabbit
10. Walrus

page 27

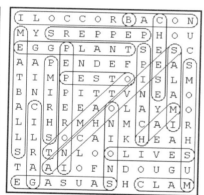

page 28

page 28-29

Extra ZZZ's, Pleeze

Answers:

1. buzz
2. jazz
3. dizzy
4. fuzzy
5. puzzle
6. buzzard
7. blizzard
8. quizzes

page 29

Answers

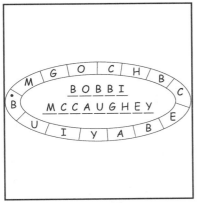

page 30

page 30

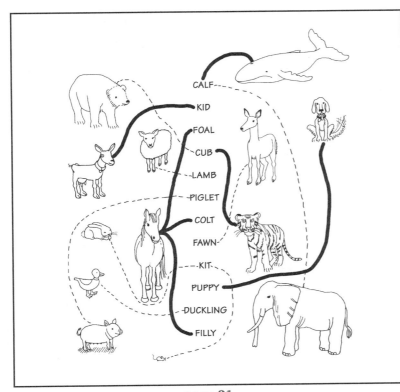

page 31

Book-ish Words

Answers:
1. BOOKEND
2. BOOKLET
3. BOOKCASE
4. BOOKMARK
5. BOOKWORM
6. BOOKPLATE
7. BOOKKEEPER
8. BOOKMOBILE
9. BOOKSELLER

page 32

Reading Rebuses

Answers:
1. Charlotte's Web
2. Goodnight Moon
3. Little House in the Big Woods
4. Curious George
5. Number the Stars
6. Harry Potter
7. Winnie-the-Pooh
8. Cat in the Hat
9. Hatchet
10. Three Little Pigs
11. Pinocchio

page 32

Answers

The Book Nook
Answers:
1. A "book crook"
2. On a "book hook"
3. A "book cook"

page 33

Oops!
Answer:
THE STINKY CHEESE MAN

page 33

A Good Mystery
Answer:
A BOOK IS A FRIEND

page 33

State Scramble
Answer:
1. Nevada
2. Idaho
3. Connecticut
4. Virginia
5. South Dakota
6. Louisiana
7. Illinois
8. New Mexico

Circled letters spell out: VACATION.

page 34

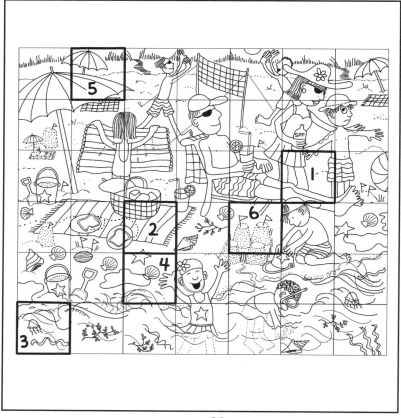

page 36

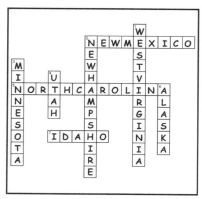

page 34

page 35

START			
SEA	SHELL	FISH	HOOK
HORSE	BACK	HAND	BALL
FLY	YARD	OUT	GAME
PAPER	STICK	BREAK	DOWN
BACK	FIRE	FAST	TOWN FINISH

page 37

Answers

page 37

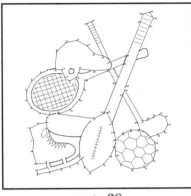

page 38

Who?

Answers:

Skate — Michelle Kwan

Golf Club — Tiger Woods

Tennis Racket — Pete Sampras

Batting Helmet — Mark McGwire

Hockey Stick — Wayne Gretzky

Football — John Elway

Soccer Ball — Mia Hamm

page 38

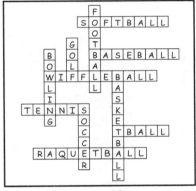

page 39

page 39

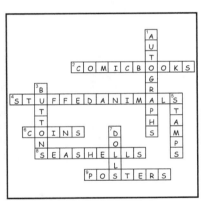

page 40

Similar Stamps

Answer: Two of the train stamps are exactly the same. Look closely — they are the two trains that have the big letter "Y" on the engine.

page 40

1 7·15·15·7·15·12 8·1·19

A G O O G O L H A S

15·14·5 8·21·14·4·18·5·4

O N E H U N D R E D

26·5·18·15·19

Z E R O S

page 42

Answers

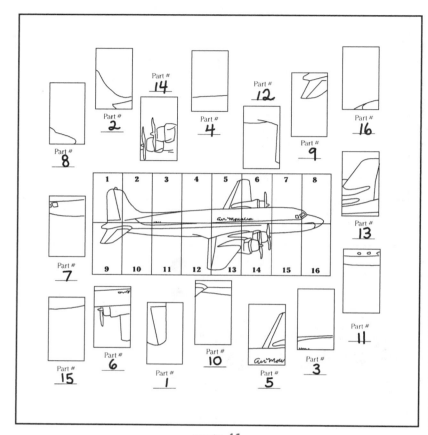

page 41

Roman Numerals

Answers:

1. If your age is 8, the Roman Numerals would be "VIII."

   If your age is 9, the Roman Numerals would be "IX."

   If your age is 10, the Roman Numerals would be "X."

   If your age is 11, the Roman Numerals would be "XI."

   If your age is 12, the Roman Numerals would be "XII."

2. The number of minutes in an hour is "LX."

3. The number of hours in a day is "XXIV."

4. The number of days in a year is "CCCLXV."

page 42

Guess who?

page 43

1. I love my computer — when it (works!)

2. Be(th ree)ked of smoke after sitting by the campfire.

3. My mother likes to w(eigh t)omatoes
   (on e)very scale in the store.

4. Annie wa(s even) early for school last week!

5. We can stu(ff our) dirty clothes in your backpack.

page 43

4	2	4	3	1	3	4	2	4
2	1	2	4	3	4	2	1	2
1	2	4	3	2	3	4	2	3
3	4	3	2	1	2	3	4	1
4	3	2	1	4	1	2	1	2
3	4	3	2	1	2	3	4	1
1	2	4	3	2	3	4	2	3
2	1	2	4	1	4	2	1	2
4	2	4	1	3	1	4	2	4

page 43

134

Answers

page 43

paper	parachute	sewing machine	telephone	bicycle
AD105	1785	1846	1876	1885

zipper	x-ray	windshield wipers	helicopter	microwave oven
1891	1895	1903	1939	1947

page 44-45

Page 4 — L
Page 6 — I
Page 9 — Q
Page 11 — U
Page 21 — I
Page 39 — D

Page 45 — P
Page 54 — A
Page 79 — P
Page 97 — E
Page 114 — R

page 44

Why Didn't I Think of That?

1. a toothbrush
2. an ice cream cone
3. a yo-yo
4. a ball-point pen
5. an airbag
6. a stethoscope
7. aspirin
8. laptop computer
9. Velcro (or hook & loop fastener)

page 45

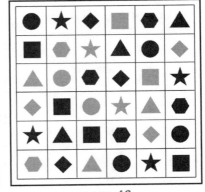

page 46

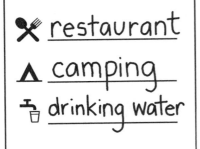

restaurant

camping

drinking water

page 46

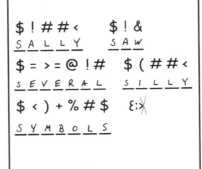

$! # # < $! &
S A L L Y   S A W

$ = > = @ ! # $ (# # <
S E V E R A L   S I L L Y

$ <) + % # $ ƐːX
S Y M B O L S

page 46

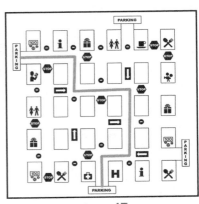

page 47

135

Answers

Idiotic Idioms

Answers:
1. cold turkey
2. get your feet wet
3. hit the books
4. on the ball
5. on the fence
6. let the cat out of the bag
7. catch some Z's

page 48

Hink Pinks

Answers:
1. happy boy = glad lad
2. not real reptile = fake snake
3. splendid group of musicians = grand band
4. a group yell = team scream
5. a skinny female ruler = lean queen
6. a large branch = big twig
7. a cold swimming place = cool pool
8. a drink at noon = lunch punch
9. a made smaller black & white animal = shrunk skunk
10. a ditch in Paris = French trench

Answer to Teeny Weeny Hink Pink: Mervin is dreaming about a "mouse house," of course!

page 49

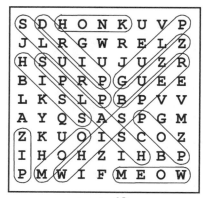

page 49

Dictionary Dissection

Possible Answers:

A	DON	RATION
ACID	DOT	RAY
ACTION	DRAIN	RID
AN	DRY	RIND
ANT	I	ROAD
ANTIC	IN	ROD
ANY	INTO	ROT
ART	ION	TAR
AT	IONIC	TIC
CAN	IOTA	TIN
CANDY	IT	TINY
CAR	NARY	TO
CART	NIT	TON
CAT	NO	TONIC
CITY	NOD	TORN
CORN	NOR	TOY
COT	NOT	TRAIN
COY	ON	TRAY
CRY	ONTO	TROD
DARN	OR	TRY
DART	RAIN	YARD
DICTION	RAN	YAR
DIN	RANT	YON
DIRTY	RAT	

page 50

Alliteration

Answers from left to right:
Clumsy Clown
Shiny Shoes
Five Fancy Fish
Two Tiny Teapots
Musical Monkey

page 50

Blended Words

Answers:
1. Breakfast + Lunch = BRUNCH
2. Flutter + Hurry = FLURRY
3. Motor + Hotel = MOTEL
4. Smack + Mash = SMASH
5. Smoke + Fog = SMOG
6. Squirm + Wiggle = SQUIGGLE
7. Twist + Whirl = TWIRL
8. Chuckle + Snort = CHORTLE

page 52

Simply Synonyms

LITTLE =	SMALL	TINY	SKIMPY	SLIGHT
WALK =	HIKE	PLOD	STROLL	STEP
FUNNY =	STRANGE	WEIRD	CURIOUS	ODD
POKE =	STAB	STICK	JAB	PROD
GROUP =	BUNCH	CLUSTER	BATCH	CROWD
STAY =	WAIT	REMAIN	STOP	LINGER
BEND =	WIND	TWIST	TURN	CURVE

page 51

Answers

Perfect Palindromes
Answers:
1. W<u>e</u> s<u>e</u>w
2. N<u>ur</u>ses r<u>u</u>n
3. St<u>e</u>p o<u>n</u> <u>n</u>o p<u>e</u>ts
4. N<u>e</u>ver <u>o</u>dd or e<u>ve</u>n

In balloon: "W<u>as</u> it <u>a</u> r<u>a</u>t I s<u>aw</u>?"

page 52

Short 'n' Sweet
Answers:
BLT = Bacon, Lettuce, and Tomato
RIP = Rest In Peace
SOS = Save Our Ship
SWAK = Sealed With A Kiss
TLC = Tender Loving Care
VIP = Very Important Person
UFO = Unidentified Flying Object
DJ = Disc Jockey
MYOB = Mind Your Own Business
ASAP = As Soon As Possible
TGIF = Thank Goodness It's Friday
SCUBA = Self-Contained Underwater
Breathing Apparatus

page 53

Recycled Words
Answers:
1. PIG - BIG - BEG - LEG
2. FOOD - FOOL - COOL - COOK
3. HAND - SAND - SEND - SEED
4. CAN - MAN - MAT - MET - BET
5. JUNK - HUNK - HONK - BONK – BANK

page 54

Don't Throw It Out
Answers:
The things that could be recycled are: newspaper, glass juice bottle, plastic milk carton, cereal box, wire coat hanger, motor oil, plastic grocery bag, magazine, tin can, cereal box, paper towel tube.
"Junk" that could be reused: clothing could be cleaned and donated, glass could be replaced in window, apple cores and dead plant could be put in compost dirt and plastic pot from plant could be used for a new plant.
Hazardous materials: oil based paint or paint with lead in it, batteries, motor oil.

page 54

page 56

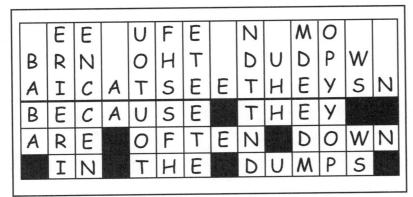

page 55

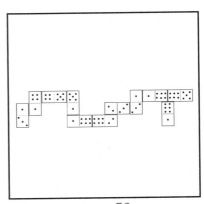

page 56

137

Answers

1. Left over after a dark brown breakfast drink is brewed. — ⓒo f f e e g r o u n d s
2. What is left after you burn logs in the fireplace. — w ⓞo d a s h e s
3. Waste matter from farm animals. — ⓜa n u r e
4. The vegetable skins that are removed before cooking. — ⓟe e l s
5. These creatures are good for the soil. — w ⓞr m s
6. These fall off trees in the fall. — l e a v e ⓢ
7. Apples, bananas, cherries, etc. — f r u i ⓣ

Mystery Word: Compost

page 55

Hopscotch Addition
Answer:
Turn One = 98 points
Turn Two = 96 points
Turn Three = 94 points
Turn Four = 92 points
Add all four turns together to get 380.

page 56

How Many Marbles?
Answer:
Sandy = 8
Peter = 10
Flo = 12

page 57

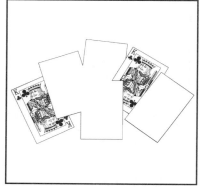

page 57

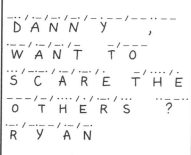

page 57

Answers to "In the Wild":

1. Spoon instead of shovel
2. Umbrella instead of pot
3. Eyeglasses instead of wood
4. Birthday candle instead of log
5. Thimble instead of bucket
6. Dice instead of stool
7. Pencil instead of fishing pole
8. Clock instead of fishing bobber
9. Pea pod instead of canoe
10. Easter basket instead of picnic basket
11. Swirly candy instead of bed roll
12. Coffee cup instead of tent
13. Playing card instead of beach towel
14. Christmas stocking instead of socks

page 58

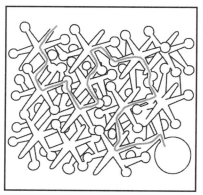

page 58

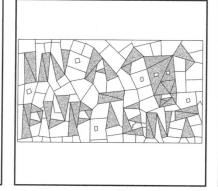

DANNY,
WANT TO
SCARE THE
OTHERS ?
RYAN

page 59

138

Answers

page 60

Emotional Exercise

Possible Answers:

				mate	moat	nit	time
				me	mole	not	tin
				mean	molt	note	tine
A	in	lime	lotion	meat	moo	oat	toe
ail	ion	line	mail	melon	moola	oil	toenail
aim	it	lint	mail	melt	moon	one	toil
ale	item	lion	mailman	men	moot	tail	tome
am	lam	lit	main	mental	motel	tail	ton
an	lame	loam	male	met	motion	tale	tonal
ant	lament	loan	malt	metal	mule	talon	tone
ate	lane	lone	man	mile	nail	tame	too
atom	late	loom	mane	mine	nail	tea	tool
eat	lean	loon	mantel	mint	name	teal	
emote	lemon	loot	mantle	mite	neat	team	
I	let	lot	mat	moan	net	tile	

page 60

page 61

How Do You Feel?

Answer: "on cloud nine"

page 61

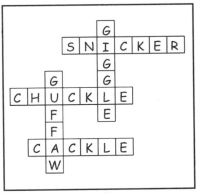

page 61

Quotabe Quote

Answers:

"No one can make you feel inferior without your consent."

A. Sing without words = HUM
B. Seven days = WEEK
C. To touch = FEEL
D. Not me = YOU
E. In a little while = SOON
F. Midday = NOON
G. Not skinny = FAT
H. Larger than a town = CITY
I. Faster than a walk = RUN
J. More pleasant = NICER
K. Not far = NEAR
L. Towards the inside = INTO

page 61

The Newlywed Name

Answers:
1. Mrs. Katie Car-Pool
2. Mrs. Franny Foot-Ball
3. Mrs. Paula Pan-Cake
4. Mrs. Julie Jelly-Fish
5. Mrs. Rita Rattle-Snake
6. Mrs. Tammy Turtle-Neck

page 62

Oh, Brother!

Answer:
Jennifer has three brothers (Billy, Tom, and Jim) and three sisters (Kathy, Therese, and Mary).

page 62

A Flurry of Families

Answers:
1. FISH live in a SCHOOL
2. LIONS live in a PRIDE
3. OXEN live in a YOKE
4. BEES live in a SWARM
5. SHEEP live in a FLOCK
6. ANTS live in a COLONY
7. GEESE live in a GAGGLE
8. DUCKS live in a BRACE
9. DOGS live in a PACK
10. CHICKS live in a CLUTCH
11. DOVES live in a COVEY
12. MONKEYS live in a TROOP
13. CLAMS live in a BED
14. RABBITS live in a DOWN
15. SWANS live in a BEVY
16. WHALES live in a POD

page 63

page 63

Answers

One Scoop—Or Two

Answer:
Nope, they are a little short of the $4.50 they would need to each get double scoops. Together the boys only have $4.35. However, they could get two double scoops, one single scoop, and have a dime leftover if they wanted to. If they were really good friends, they would figure out a way to share the extra two scoops between the three of them!

page 64

Share & Share Alike

Answer:
The boys decide to make applesauce!

page 64

page 64

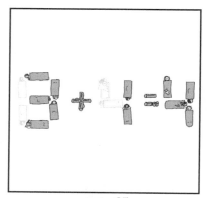

page 65

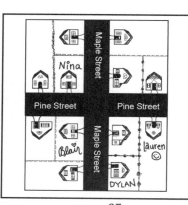

page 65

Household Words

Answers:
1. HOUSEFLY
2. HOUSEBOAT
3. HOUSEHOLD
4. HOUSEWORK
5. HOUSEPLANT
6. HOUSEKEEPER

page 66

At Home Wherever They Go

Answers:
1. SNAIL
2. HERMIT CRAB
3. TURTLE
4. BACKPACKER

page 66

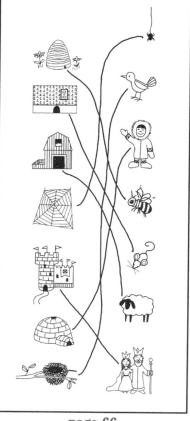

page 66

Answers

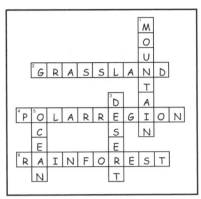

page 67

page 68

Keyboard Code
Answer:
Find each letter and number of the secret message on the keyboard. Now for each one, locate the key in the next row down and slightly to the right. When you do this you will find that Charles Babbage's nickname is "THE FATHER OF COMPUTERS."

page 68

Dumb Deletions
Answers:
1. Virtual Virus
2. Double Data
3. Perfect Password

page 69

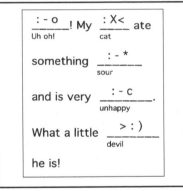

page 69

page 69

Subject Scramble
Answers to scrambled words:
1. READING
2. SCIENCE
3. MATHEMATICS
4. PHYS. ED.
5. SOCIAL STUDIES

Answer to circled letters: RECESS

page 70

page 70

page 71

141

Answers

Hot Lunch
Answer:
Pizza and water.

page 71

page 71

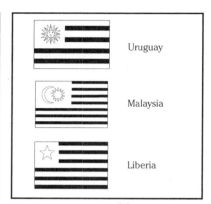

Uruguay

Malaysia

Liberia

page 72

Hello Friend
Answer:
The letter reads: Hi! My name is Rudolpho. I have 10 years** and live in Brazil. I like to sing and to play guitar. What do you like to do? Please write to me SOON! Your new friend, Rudolpho.

**In many countries, people say that they "have" a certain number of years instead of they "are" a certain number of years old.

page 72

page 73

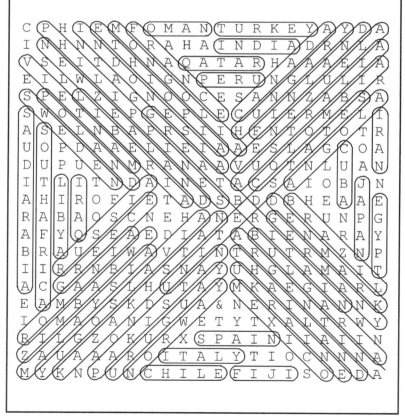

page 73

Answers

Shell Talk
Answer:
There is a lot to see under the sea!

page 74

School of Fish
Answer:
There are 82 fish in the school that stretches across both pages. Actually, there are 83 if you add the one little fish which is scared of the submarine!

page 74-75

What's Dot?
Both a submarine and an octopus travel under the sea.

page 75

page 74-75

Missing Parts
Answers:
1. WIZARD
2. KNIGHT
3. UNICORN
4. TROLL
5. FAIRIES
6. GNOME
7. DRAGON
8. PRINCESS

page 76

A Corner Castle
Answer:
There are 65 basic squares and rectangles that make up this castle. However, if you start to count the outline of squares and rectangles of the same size that are next to each other as an additional shape, the total is MUCH higher! For example: If you count the right-hand tower the "basic" way, you get 20 rectangles; if you count it the "overlapping" way, you get 39. Try it and see!

page 76

THERE ISN'T MUSHROOM!

page 76

page 77

Answers

page 78

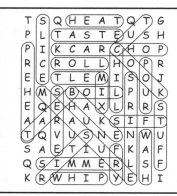

page 78

Totally Tablespoons
Answer:
Flour = 32 Tbsp.
Sugar = 24 Tbsp.
Cocoa = 4 Tbsp.

page 78

Mystery Meals
Answers:
The recipes (from top to bottom on the page) are for chocolate chip cookies, green salad, macaroni and cheese, French toast.

page 79

Seeing Double
Answers:
1. AARDVARK
2. KANGAROO
3. MONGOOSE
4. RABBIT
5. OPOSSUM
6. GIRAFFE
7. GIBBON
8. HIPPO
9. PARROT

page 80

page 80

page 81

144

Answers

page 82

Hiding in a Honeycomb

Answers to Hiding in a Honeycomb: ant, bee, beetle, fly, flea, ladybug

page 83

BUTTERFLY to
FLY PAPER to
PAPERBACK to
BACKFIRE to
FIREFLY

page 83

Itsy Bitsy

Answer:
A spider walking on a mirror!

page 83

Charlotte's Riddle

Answer:
Their webbing day!

page 83

Tools of the Trade

Hiding in the garden are a teakettle, a plate of bacon and eggs, a pizza slice, needle and thread, a spool of thread, a blender, a chair, and a kite.

page 84

Bee to Flower

Answer: Stare at the dark line between the bee and the flower for several seconds. Now, keep staring at the line and slowly bring the picture close to your face. See what happens?

page 84

Answers

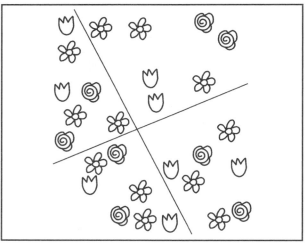

page 84

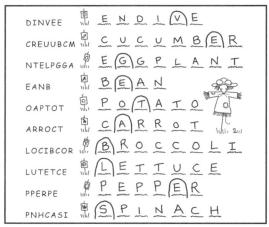

DINVEE — ENDIVE
CREUUBCM — CUCUMBER
NTELPGGA — EGGPLANT
EANB — BEAN
OAPTOT — POTATO
ARROCT — CARROT
LOCIBCOR — BROCCOLI
LUTETCE — LETTUCE
PPERPE — PEPPER
PNHCASI — SPINACH

page 85

CHIVE BASIL DILL MINT PARSLEY

page 85

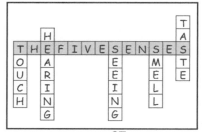

THE FIVE SENSES
HEARING
TOUCH
SEEING
SMELL
TASTE

page 87

Body Scramble

Answers:
OTES = TOES #9
SWAIT = WAIST #5
GLES = LEGS #7
CKNE = NECK #2
DAEH = HEAD #1
STECH = CHEST #4
SHIP HIPS #6
EFET = FEET #8
DOSHULRES = SHOULDERS #3

page 87

Say What?

Answers:
The three tiny bones deep inside your ear are the smallest in your body. All three of them could fit on the nail of your pinky finger with room to spare! These tiny bones have an important job to do—they pass sound vibrations from your eardrum to a special nerve that goes to your brain. Then your brain makes sense out of all the noises you are hearing.

page 87

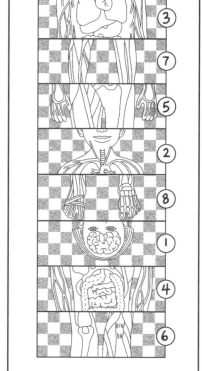

page 86

Answers

page 88

	Mostly Sunny
	Emergency Weather
A+	Terrific Day
	Emergency Weather
	Overcast
	Rainy
	Overcast
	Light Wind
	Overcast
	Gusts Of Wind
	Ice and Sleet
	Sunny
A+	Terrific Day

page 89

page 90

5 Drop books at library.
4 Pick up pie at bakery.
2 Get mail at post office.
1 Pick up paper at computer store.
3 Buy flea soap at pet store.
6 Get milk at grocery store.

thanks! ♡♡♡MOM   Do this last!

page 91

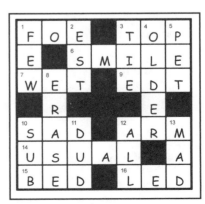

page 92

Answers

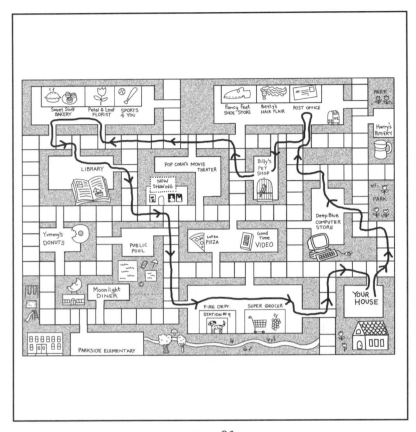

page 91

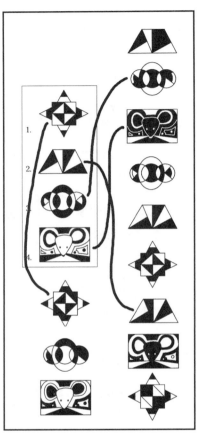

page 93

Say Again?

Answers:

"Hey there, Jason."

"Hello, Aaron!"

"How are you?"

"I have a bad cold."

"How terrible! I hope you get better soon."

"Me, too. I didn't sleep all night long."

"Oh, that's too bad."

"Well, I have to go. Goodbye!"

"Goodbye. See you later."

page 93

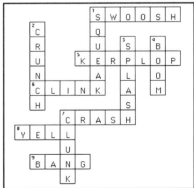

page 94

page 94

Answers

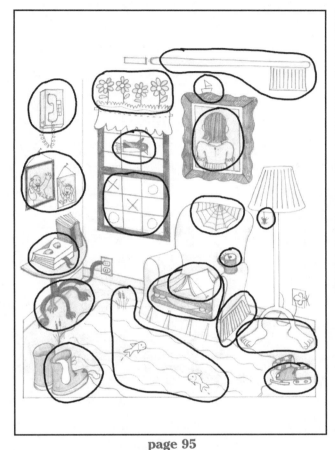

page 95

Crossword answers:

2. SACKRACE
3. PEANUTONASPOONRELAY
4. EGGTOSS
7. CAPTURETHEFLAG
9. LIMBO
11. HOTPOTATO
14. PINTHETAILONTHEDONKEY
15. SIMONSAYS
16. PINATA
17. THREELEGGEDRACE
18. WHEELBARROWRACE

Down:
1. FREEZE
5. GIANT
6. BOBBINGFORAPPLES
10. MUSICALCHAIRS
12. FOOTBALL
13. TELEPHONELINE
3. PAGE
8. TUGOFWAR

page 97

Calling Code
Answers:

1. IMA NUTT
2. FRANK N STEIN
3. TED E BEAR
4. TAFFY PULL
5. DREW A BOAT
6. SUMMER TIME
7. SANTA CLAUS

page 96

"What's Wrong"?
1. Phone is too high
2. Two pictures are talking to each other
3. Book on table has eyes and tongue
4. Table has animal feet and tail
5. Boot is a dog
6. Rug is a pond
7. Slipper is a snowmobile
8. Floor lamp has bare feet
9. Spider is the chain for the lamp
10. Spider web is the lace doily on the chair
11. Mug has an eye
12. Magazine on the chair is a tent
13. Chair cushion is a sandwich
14. Ruffle on side of chair is a comb
15. Portrait of girl shows the back of her head
16. Small boat is sailing on the picture frame
17. Toothbrush is molding and air conditioning vent
18. Flowers are growing out of the curtains
19. Tic-tac-toe game on the window panes
20. Penguin is flying past the window

page 95

page 96

Answers

I Can't Believe My Eyes

Answers:

1. You see a number 13 or a capital letter B depending on which way you read, left to right, or top to bottom. Visually, the letters and numbers are so similar that the figure in the middle tricks your eyes and can be read either way.
2. The long black lines are parallel to each other. Take a ruler and measure to see that this is true. The short lines that go in different directions fool your eyes into thinking that the long lines are crooked.
3. This is perhaps one of the most famous optical puzzles. It is called the "Rubin Vase." You can see either two dark faces or a white vase depending on which color and shape you concentrate.
4. All the girls are exactly the same height! The perspective lines in the background fool your eye into thinking the girl on the right is the tallest.
5. This is an "impossible" drawing! There are either four planks or three planks depending on which end of the pile you are looking at.

6. Between the three bunnies they only have three ears!
7. Both lines are the same length. Measure them to see that this is true. The short, slanting lines at the end of the longer lines fools your eyes into thinking the top line is longer.
8. Try tilting the book so this page is at eye level, as if you were looking across the top of a table. The secret message is "HELLO!" Once you see the message with the page tilted, it is easy to figure out how the squares and lines make up the letters. Can you figure out how to write other secret messages this way?
9. You might have to twist your vision a little, but this hexagon can also be seen as a transparent cube. Try lightly shading two of the triangles that are right next to each other. This will help you to see one of the "sides" of the cube.
10. You should see flashing grey dots where the white lines cross. What's really interesting is that if you look directly at a grey spot, it disappears!
11. Even though the white triangle is not really there, your mind fills in the space between the three dots so that you "see" the triangle.

page 98-99

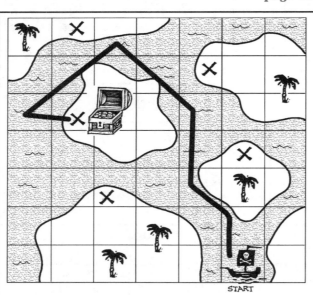

page 100

Dividing the Booty

Answer:
Captain Jack gets 25 coins
One-Eyed Pete gets 10 coins
Barnacle Bill gets 5 coins
Peg-Leg Larry gets 10 coins

page 101

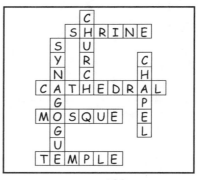

page 102

Household Chores

Answers:
1. SWEEP floor
2. WASH dishes
3. SET table
4. VACUUM rugs
5. DUST furniture
6. RECYCLE newspapers
7. EMPTY trash cans
8. FOLD laundry
9. SCRUB sink
10. WATER plants
11. COOK meals
12. FEED pets

page 102

Walk the Plank

Answers:
1. A pirate would probably not deposit his money in a <u>BANK</u>.
2. Stealing a pirate's wooden leg and replacing it with an umbrella might be considered a <u>PRANK</u>.
3. Pirates probably <u>STANK</u> because they couldn't bathe very often.
4. On board a pirate ship they might use a <u>CRANK</u> to turn a wheel.
5. If pirates <u>DRANK</u> sea water they would get really sick.
6. Many pirate ships <u>SANK</u> during a bad storm or after a battle.

page 101

Answers

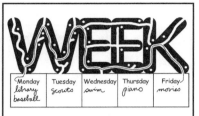

page 103

page 104

Having Fun
Answers:
1. FLY KITE
2. EAT FOOD
3. READ BOOK
4. TAKE NAP
5. WALK DOG
6. CLIMB TREE
7. THROW BALL
8. PLAY CARDS

page 106

page 105

page 104

page 105

1. B L A N K E T
2. S A N D W I C H E S
3. C H I P S
4. N A P K I N S
5. L E M O N A D E
6. F R U I T

Answer: P I C N I C
B A S K E T

page 106

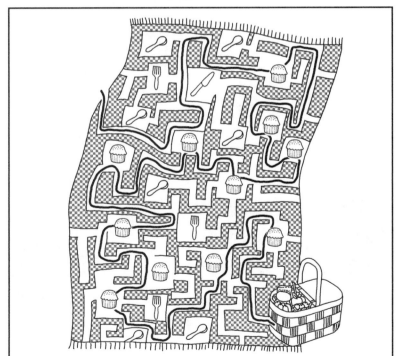

page 107

151

Answers

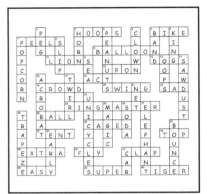

page 108

Clowning Around

Answers:
1. Tiny hat becomes a hermit crab.
2. Wig becomes a sheep.
3. Rubber nose becomes a clock.
4. Painted mouth becomes a banana.
5. Bow tie becomes a butterfly.
6. Baggy suit becomes a baggy elephant, seal, hippo, and snake.
7. Squirting flower squirts into an umbrella!
8. Horn becomes the head of a duck. The edge of the baggy suit and the pocket becomes the body of the duck.
9. Big shoes become a fish and an alligator.

page 109

Tricky Tongue Twisters

Answers:
1. Elegant Elephants
2. Jolly Jugglers Jiggle Jelly Jars
3. Two Tawny Tigers Travel Twitching Tightropes Together
4. Aerial Acrobats Accomplish Absolutely Amazing Acts Above An Awestruck Audience

page 109

Word Wheel

Answer: Because they are tired!

page 110

Tallest Tree

Answer: It is a giant Sequoia that stands three hundred and sixty five feet tall — wow! That's tall!

page 112

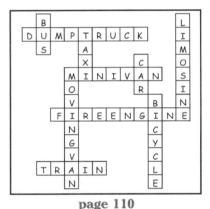

page 110

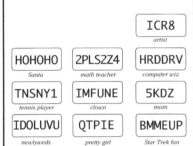

page 111

Properly Pronounced

Answers:
1. MAPLE
2. BEECH
3. OAK
4. SPRUCE
5. BIRCH
6. PALM
7. WILLOW
8. FIR
9. JUNIPER
10. MAHOGANY
11. POPLAR
12. CEDAR
13. BALSAM
14. HICKORY

page 112

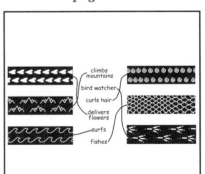

page 111

page 113

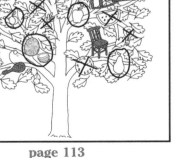

page 114

Answers

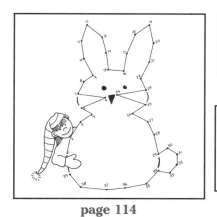

page 114

Hot Chocolate
Answer:
Jon = 0, Keith = 6, and Adam = 3

page 114

Snowy Words
Answers:
1. snowball
2. snowflake
3. snowman
4. snowmobile
5. snowshoes
6. snowplow
7. snowstorm

page 115

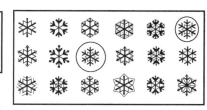

page 115

Merry Poppin'
Answers:
1. Popeye
2. Poplar
3. Poppy
4. Popular
5. Popsicle

page 116

Mystery Menu
Answer:
Read all the capital letters in the menu to find the following hidden message —
TWO SODAS FOR THE PRICE OF ONE

page 116

One Bird or Two
Answer:
A bird in the hand is worth two in the bush.

page 118

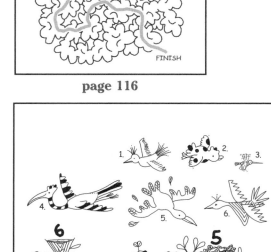

page 116

page 117

page 118

Answers

Sunflower Snack

Answers:
1. Cardinal
2. Chickadee
3. Blue Jay
4. Tufted Titmouse
5. Grackle
6. Sparrow
7. Finch
8. Nuthatch
9. Woodpecker

page 119

Two Way Ducks

Answer:
Simply take your thumb and cover the head of the end duck. If you cover the duck's head all the way to the left, the ducks appear to waddle to the right. If you cover the duck's head all the way to the right, the ducks waddle back to the left!

page 119

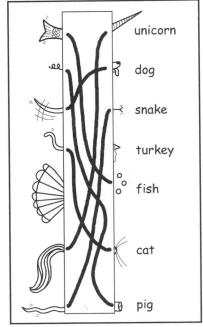

page 120

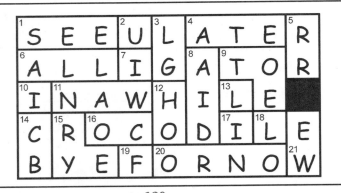

page 120

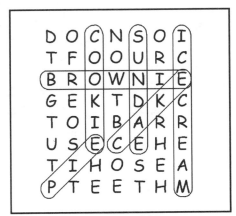

page 121

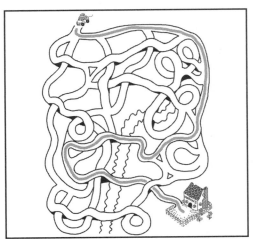

page 121